GREAT AMERICAN FOOD

GREAT

AMERICAN FOOD
Charlie Palmer
with Judith Choate

Photography by
Gozen Koshida

RANDOM
HOUSE
NEW YORK

*I dedicate this book to the memories of Joyce and Dwight
and to the future with Lisa, Courtland, and Randall.*
CHARLIE

———

*With gratitude to Charlie's mom who I never got to meet
but who I felt looking over my shoulder from the minute I
began working on this book.*
JUDIE

THANKS AND APPRECIATION

Joel Avirom and his team

Mickey Choate

Juan DeLeon

Jason Epstein and his team

Alex Gouras

Hiromi Hayashi

Gozen Koshida

Susan Lescher

Richard LoPuzzo

Steve Pool

Nicky Reeves

Joe Romano

Dan Rundell

Marc Sarrazin

Michael Valle

and the staffs of
Aureole, Lenox Room, and Alva

CONTENTS

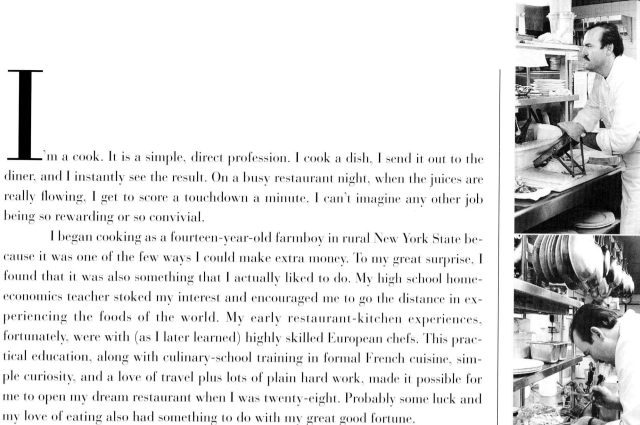

I'm a cook. It is a simple, direct profession. I cook a dish, I send it out to the diner, and I instantly see the result. On a busy restaurant night, when the juices are really flowing, I get to score a touchdown a minute. I can't imagine any other job being so rewarding or so convivial.

I began cooking as a fourteen-year-old farmboy in rural New York State because it was one of the few ways I could make extra money. To my great surprise, I found that it was also something that I actually liked to do. My high school home-economics teacher stoked my interest and encouraged me to go the distance in experiencing the foods of the world. My early restaurant-kitchen experiences, fortunately, were with (as I later learned) highly skilled European chefs. This practical education, along with culinary-school training in formal French cuisine, simple curiosity, and a love of travel plus lots of plain hard work, made it possible for me to open my dream restaurant when I was twenty-eight. Probably some luck and my love of eating also had something to do with my great good fortune.

From the beginning, I have been able to encounter all kinds of food in the raw. I've grown vegetables, slaughtered animals, caught fish, hunted truffles, and harvested grapes. I have tried to understand where all the food that we eat comes from and translate its heritage into complementary tastes at the table. Fortunately, there is nothing I won't eat, so I have a broad spectrum of experiences and foods from which I can create new recipes.

I feel very lucky to be able to make a living doing something that I really love. I daydream about juicy, succulent squab, delicate, silken scallops, and molten chocolate, and then I get to make my dreams come true in the kitchen. Not only do I get to eat great food, I also get the immediate satisfaction that comes from feeding people well.

My particular style of cooking is based on culinary *tradition* with a strong infusion of classical French cuisine. Along with this foundation, *seasonality* carries great importance because, to me, it sparks the feelings and memories associated with comfortable dining. Fall and winter bring forth hearty, body-and-soul-warming dishes such as soups, reduction sauces, risottos, grains, and aromatic roasts. Spring means simple grilled fish, warm vinaigrettes instead of sauces, bouillons infused with herbs, flavored oils, and pan juices. Of course spring, and then summer, offer tons of fruits and vegetables to kindle the imagination. Then comes *taste*. Every dish I cook begins with a clear sense of taste. Once this is established, I bring together all the components of the dish to intensify this basic flavor. I believe that one must al-

INTRODUCTION

ways keep the essence of the main ingredient the focal point of a dish. If it is quail, then quail must be the taste that prevails; the other components are there only to heighten the flavor and texture and to catch the juices and distribute them onto the tongue with balanced complexity.

I also believe that there are some foods so pure and so distinct in flavor that they often require no addition to punctuate their delicacy. To me, caviar, oysters, and soft-shell crabs always shine on their own. When serving these foods without adornment, you should always buy the best and then serve them simply, with just a bit of an acidic jolt to heighten the natural aromas.

Finally, I think about *display*. There is no doubt that people eat with their eyes as well as their mouths. Presentation is, to me, an integral part of the art of cooking. I like to look at the foods I prepare in a playful way and create excitement for the diner. Eating is an everyday occurrence, but imagination will make great dining special. I like to think that my food concepts are in a constant state of growth. Each day ideas grow and evolve into what I think are unique menus—usually a bit sophisticated yet approachable and, I hope, honest.

My recipes are a definite extension of my personality. There is no denying that I am a big American guy with a heritage of many nationalities. I love the outdoors, sports, my family. I find the abundance of contemporary American life invigorating and a great stimulus to my culinary adventures. With such bounty and quality surrounding us, there is no reason that the American kitchen can't produce the world's best dishes.

In my kitchen, this translates into rambunctious, intense flavors, unexpected combinations, superb ingredients, substantial portions, and flavors and displays that will make the diner sit up and take notice. The excitement begins in the kitchen but culminates at the table. The pride that I feel when the bold design of food carefully placed on beautiful china combines with the savory aromas to entice the diner to experience the sensual tastes that we have created is as thrilling to me as are the discoveries in the kitchen.

I sincerely believe that good cooking is 85 percent applied common sense. If you really understand the flavors, the tastes, and the look that you want to achieve in a particular dish, you can easily create them. Of course, the 15 percent that is creativity will often make the difference between the extra effort a good cook puts into making a good meal and what a great cook invents to create a great one. I would hope that this book will demystify the "secrets" of great cooking for you so that you can nurture your desire to be a great cook.

In order to speed the home cook's understanding of great cooking, I have chosen a home cook to help me put this book together. Although Judie Choate has cooked professionally, she was not trained as a chef. Her style of cooking is, therefore, in the tradition of the mother in the kitchen. Rather like the expediter in our

restaurant kitchens, whose task it is to see that everyone is doing his or her job to get the meals out at the proper pace, it has been Judie's job to translate my methods and ideas to the home kitchen. Together we have tried to make the dishes simple to cook and inexpensive to re-create as well as healthful to eat.

Throughout the book I frequently offer wine suggestions to complete a dish. These are not the requisite bottles but those that both reflect my palate and balance the flavors of my food. I encourage you to try these wines and also to seek out those vintners and vintages that complement the food to your individual taste.

For me, the preparation of food and the eating of it are immediate satisfactions. If you purchase the best and the freshest and then allow your mind to concentrate on the taste you want to create at the table, the fun will begin. Cook it and then serve it "just picked," "piping hot," "when the juices are still retained inside the crust," "layered on a mixture of baby greens," or whatever the recipe demands. Just make it the best. Together, let's follow the seasons, investigate both the old foods and the new, and then share our love of good cooking. I know you will find that *Great American Food* can be made just as easily in your kitchen as in mine.

CHARLIE PALMER

A t Aureole the main kitchen is located at the back of the restaurant, across a narrow corridor from the upstairs dining room. When you take the two steps across this passageway and push through the double swinging doors, you could easily be forgiven for thinking that you had been transported to another dimension. From the tranquility of the elegant dining room, those two steps and quick push hurl you into a minifactory running full-out.

The first and most immediate contrast with the dining room is the sound. In the dining room, fine wines are quietly discussed and plates whisked to and from the table with a minimum of effort, while the kitchen is *loud*. Ice machines continuously whir and clatter, producing the enormous quantities of ice necessary for all restaurant operations; dishwashers and pot-scrubbing machines slam and bump; and the actual cooking supplies its own constant throb. Pots, sauté pans, and saucepans are flung at breakneck speed to ready the incoming stream of orders. Though this kitchen often looks and sounds like a demolition derby, it is not a deliberate attempt to bang and make noise but kitchen efficiency that creates the havoc. The food-preparation stations are close together. As in a submarine, there is no wasted space. All this allows the food to pass from the raw state to a finished, mouth-watering plate in an unbelievably short time.

The line cooks, herded by the sous chef, work furiously. "Oui oui, sir" is their only answer to orders called and questions asked. The orders fly in: "2 veal, 3 crabs, 7 ravioli, a soup, 1 squab, 3 beef— 2 medium, 1 rare, sos" (sauce on the side). Once in a while one hears a "What'sa matter, you need a recipe?" or a "Speed it up, this *is* for tonight!" Hands and arms are seared along with the meat. On and on, for two seatings at lunch and three seatings at dinner, the orders, the abuse, the compliments. Time goes fast, then faster.

Charlie stands at one end of the outside line, simultaneously shredding potatoes for the scallop sandwiches, expediting the sequence of orders from the dining room, directing the timing so that each table's order is ready to be placed in front of each diner at the same time, and eagle-eyeing every plate that passes through the counter. There is not much talking and little time for it in any case.

IF YOU CAN'T STAND THE HEAT . . .
24 HOURS IN A RESTAURANT KITCHEN

The only voice heard above the noise is Charlie's, urging and encouraging his kitchen brigade on and barking out the orders in the staccato code that is the lingua franca of a professional kitchen operating at this level.

The dishwashers work steadily, ensuring that there is an ample supply of clean cooking equipment and sparkling dishes stacked in front of the cooks.

Nothing is wasted, especially time. When there is a lull between service, each cook, even Charlie, picks up and continues whatever task was assigned early in the day. When one job is finished, another begins. It seems that the kitchen can never catch up with the demands on its services. Time is always short.

There are no leftovers. Anything that can be is incorporated into the rich stocks in the ongoing stockpot. Bits and pieces are incorporated into the "family meal," which feeds the staff twice a day. Any excess becomes the basis for new recipes to be tested. The traditional French kitchen economy is always the rule. Both time and ingredients are expensive, and their careful expenditure controls the cost of running a fine restaurant—a never-ending concern for Charlie and his crew.

The kitchen is very hot. It should be, with stoves, oven, broilers, fryers, and a sixty-gallon stockpot working at all times. In fact, the combination of the open, blooming fires, the movement of cooks and food, and the steady, low roar does bring that other hot, confined place to mind. Incorporate the flame into the noise and perhaps Charlie is an earthbound Vulcan and the kitchen is his forge.

Always enter or leave the kitchen through the door on your right. Push through and move off quickly. And don't saunter—you may be run over or nudged aside with a quiet but firm "excuse me." Sightseeing is a luxury reserved for the dining room.

If the kitchen is the heartbeat of the restaurant, the front-of-the-house staff are its arteries. The captains, waiters, and busboys are directed by the very suave maitre d', Alex Gouras. Their deft hands ensure that guests dine in quiet splendor. And, on those occasions when too many orders hit too fast and the kitchen's slammin', the diner will feel none of the chaos. Just as the cooks have chosen a highly disciplined profession, so too have the service personnel. So the beat goes on.

All of this activity begins at five every morning, except on Sunday, when Richard LoPuzzo, the executive sous chef, unlocks the basement entrance doors. There is no one quite like Richard—he truly is a wizard. Once he opens the door, he will have only a few minutes of quiet before the purveyors begin their deliveries and

the kitchen staff and cooks begin arriving. In those few minutes, Richard will sense the condition of the dining rooms and the kitchen, will know what raw materials will be needed to bring them to life, and, most important, will know who has been naughty and who has been nice.

He is father confessor, disciplinarian, timekeeper, and Charlie's right-hand man. He knows everything before anyone else in the restaurant. He needs his few moments of morning quiet. Those few minutes of solitude will end with a bang as the basement door begins admitting the first entrants into the kitchen family. The day cooks and prep people suit up into their black-and-white checkered pants and white coats and immediately go to work, peeling, cutting, chopping, boning, mixing, slicing, carving, sautéing—all the kitchen techniques you can imagine are in full use by 6:00 A.M. Richard has already begun his litany of "beautiful," "lovely," and "whadda *you* want?" that will be repeated hundreds of times before he leaves, on a good day, at 6:00 P.M.

The two defined kitchen areas at Aureole are too small to contain the myriad preparations that must come together by 5:30 P.M., when the first dinner guests arrive. Makeshift tables line the hallways, and intense young cooks wrapped in their own worlds of the *art culinaire* will be found peeling, shelling, coring, and carving their daily mandates.

The downstairs kitchen is crammed with work stations. It is here that the pastry chef, Dan Rundell, runs his tight ship. Grousing, cajoling, and screaming, the normally taciturn young artist elicits miracles from his crew. The butcher, the pasta makers, the pâté and terrine prep cooks, and anyone else who can find a spot also work here. A dishwasher bangs, scrubs, shines, and bangs some more. The huge walk-in refrigerator is a common denominator for everyone. Knock. "I'm going in." Knock. "I'm out," and Richard's "whadda *you* want?" echo over the parade.

In a small office cubby, Juan DeLeon, the steward in charge of ordering, is never off the phone: "Only the best"; "Why did you send us that junk?"; "Take it back"; "Bring me fresh . . . of course today!"; What fish are in—are they great, the best? If they aren't, don't bother, you keep 'em." And so it goes all day long, as the restaurant demands only the finest the market has to offer.

Charlie arrives at midmorning to scan the scene. His orders, plans, ideas, and final decisions get discussed. He checks over everyone working. He demonstrates new recipes, talks over the previous night's service, and corrects mistakes. He generally speaks softly, even when dissatisfied. But occasionally, his six-foot-four-inch frame bellows. And, even more rarely, his powerful temper explodes when he feels that the reputation of the restaurant has been hurt. His day will end after midnight, as the last diners are biting into their after-dinner chocolate truffles.

Charlie demands that each plate be sent out as though it were to be judged by Escoffier. He knows that the diners are guests in his dining room and deserve only the very best he can offer. Nothing less will please him, and he must be pleased before a plate goes out to the dining room. He knows that for many of his guests an evening at Aureole is an event, a special occasion, a not-to-be-forgotten treat. And it always is!

At some point in every service, Charlie unties his work apron and heads for the dining room. It is not the accolades of the diners he seeks but the quiet smiles of contentment that tell him that his kitchen, once again, has delivered what he has promised.

Coming into this world is like being adopted by a huge, overpowering family. The warmth of the crew is almost as overwhelming as the heat of the kitchen itself. For almost three years I was a part of this private world as I peeked over shoulders and got in the way, learning Charlie's techniques and style so that I could translate them for the home cook. I occasionally saw tempers flare, but mostly I felt the generosity of sharing. When their learning experience at Aureole came to an end, line cooks and sous chefs were happily sent on their way to new adventures. Recipes and new dining spots were talked over and argued about like a teenager's gossip fest. Romances bloomed—Joey and Meghan got married. Babies were born, including Charlie's two glorious sons. Pipes burst, air-conditioning failed, the dining room was flooded just after it had been totally refurbished, and still, every night at 5:30, the lights dim, the flowers open, the silver gleams, and the first guests of the evening enter the peacefully peachy and glowing dining room. And, once again, across the two steps and through the double doors, the maelstrom is full-out.

Bon apetit!
JUDIE CHOATE

GREAT
AMERICAN
FOOD

I. CELEBRATING THE FIRST COURSE: APPETIZERS AND SOUPS

Appetizers should never overwhelm but should complement the tastes to come. Often the first course serves to entice the diner with a bit of luxury. Traditional appetizers, dating from the period of minimal refrigeration, when perishable food was rare, were frequently as unassuming as broiled grapefruit, melon, or avocado, in season, but often as extravagant as the seafood cocktails, oysters on the half shell, and smoked fish that still rate high on my menu. Each of these quietly and deliciously notified diners that extra care had been taken to serve them well.

Great soups are frequently the prelude to a great dinner and, according to the French masters, are to be considered the "soul of the dinner." Served as a first course after passed hors d'oeuvres or, in a very formal service, after an appetizer and before the fish course, soups can also be the focus around which a light supper or lunch is formed. In a restaurant setting, soup is usually eaten as an appetizer, often with a glass of well-balanced Chardonnay.

Although there are hundreds of soups, each of them can be classified into one of four categories: broths, clear soups, thick soups, and purees. Regardless of type, soups should reflect the tastes and offset the flavors and colors of the rest of the meal.

Of all the enticements that excite the appetite, I can think of none as luxurious as foie gras. I can remember, as if it were yesterday, the first time that I ate this fabulously rich treat: It was in France, I was nineteen, and boy did I think it was weird-tasting stuff. I was amazed to find myself an addict almost at once. Little did I know that foie gras would become such an important part of my restaurant repertoire. Foie gras is truly an indulgence, rich in every sense. Fine-quality livers cost about forty dollars a pound, and each tablespoon represents sixty calories of protein and saturated fat. But for special-occasion meals, I feel that it is a worthwhile indulgence.

Since the appetizer is often the first opportunity you have to dazzle your guests, you should display your best effort. If you don't have time to create a complex terrine or a plate with many components, do something as simple as the Lobster (or Shrimp

Foie Gras Mousse served lakeside at
Michael Ginor's Hudson Valley Foie Gras Farm.

or Crab) Cocktail with Light Lemon Sabayon (page 18) or even some sparkling-fresh oysters with Red Wine Mignonette (page 196). Just make sure that, whatever it is, it is the absolute best you can create. For the best will only sharpen your guests' appetites for the meal to come.

APPETIZERS

Grilled and Roasted Vegetable Terrine

Slow-Roasted Beet and Goat Cheese Gâteau

Roasted Asparagus with Parma Ham and Roasted Pepper Coulis

Foie Gras Terrine

Foie Gras Mousse

Sautéed Escalopes of Foie Gras with Savory Corn Cakes

Lobster Cocktail with Light Lemon Sabayon

Sea Scallop Sandwiches with Citrus Juices

Crab Lasagna with Tomato-Basil Coulis

Pepper-Seared Salmon and New Potato Terrine with Spring Leeks

Warm New Potato Blinis with Seared Salmon, Cultured Cream, and Osetra Caviar

Pepper-Seared Haddock and "Brandade" Cake with Warm Black Truffle Vinaigrette

Sesame-Seared Tuna Cake with Mustard Vinaigrette

Spice-Seared Cervena Venison with Apple-Turnip Conserve, Marinated Leeks, and Caramel Jus

SOUPS

Wild Mushroom Minestrone with Mascarpone Dumplings

Butternut Squash Soup

Chilled Beefsteak Tomato Soup with Goat Cheese Croutons

New Potato and Leek Potage with Oregon Morels

Cold Lobster and Sauternes Cream

Grilled and Roasted
Vegetable Terrine

Makes one 12-inch terrine

Although this recipe seems long and involved, it really is simple. You will speed along if, in true restaurant-chef's fashion, you organize all of your ingredients and prepare each one before assembling the terrine. Since it needs to set for 8 hours, this terrine is a perfect dinner-party appetizer. It also shines at a cocktail buffet, served with crisp toast triangles.

1 ½ cups olive oil
¾ cup balsamic vinegar
Coarse salt
Pepper
4 large artichokes
Juice of 1 lemon
3 large eggplants
1 large zucchini
1 large yellow squash
2 large or 4 medium Portobello mushrooms
3 red bell peppers
3 yellow bell peppers
2 leeks
2 ½ tablespoons unflavored gelatin
4 cups Vegetable Stock (page 190)
1 teaspoon minced fresh chervil
1 teaspoon minced fresh parsley
1 teaspoon minced fresh tarragon
1 teaspoon minced fresh thyme
1 teaspoon minced fresh chives

Combine olive oil, vinegar, and salt and pepper to taste. Set aside.

Trim and stem the artichokes and remove any blemished parts. Place in a medium saucepan with cold water to cover, lemon juice, and salt to taste. Lay a heavy kitchen towel on top of the pan and cover with a heatproof plate to keep artichokes under the water. Place over high heat and bring to a boil. Lower heat and simmer for 30 minutes, or until artichokes are tender. Drain well and allow to rest until cool enough to handle. Carefully trim off all leaves and scrape out choke (the fuzzy interior) with a teaspoon, leaving a nicely shaped bottom. Cover and reserve.

Wash eggplants, zucchini, and yellow squash and remove any blemishes. Trim stem ends. Cut, lengthwise, into ¼-inch-thick slices, discarding end pieces. You will need 10 slices of eggplant and 5 slices each of zucchini and yellow squash. Place veg-

A NOTE FROM CHARLIE

So many restaurant diners request vegetarian meals that we must constantly devise nonmeat courses. This terrine is full of the intense flavor I demand from all of my recipes.

etables in a shallow dish and pour in ½ cup of olive-oil mixture. Toss to coat and marinate for 1 hour.

Trim stems from mushrooms and reserve for another use. Wipe mushrooms clean. Place in a shallow bowl, add ½ cup of the olive-oil mixture, and marinate for 1 hour.

Preheat grill or broiler.

Place whole peppers on a hot grill (or under the broiler). Grill, turning frequently, for about 5 minutes, or until skins have blackened. Remove from grill and place in a plastic container with lid or a plastic bag with a tie, and let steam for about 5 minutes, or until skins can be pushed off easily. Remove and discard the skins. Carefully split peppers open. Remove and discard stems, seeds, and membranes. Lay the peppers, interior sides down, on a paper towel to drain. Reserve each color separately.

Preheat the oven to 350°F.

Place eggplant, zucchini, and yellow squash on preheated grill. Grill, turning frequently, for about 4 minutes, or until cooked through but not mushy. Place eggplant, zucchini, and yellow squash in separate shallow containers with ¼ cup of the olive-oil mixture, tossing to coat. Set aside.

Place mushrooms on a baking sheet in preheated oven and roast for 5 minutes. Remove from oven and toss with 2 tablespoons of the olive-oil mixture. Reserve.

Combine artichoke hearts and ¼ cup of the olive-oil mixture, tossing to coat. Set aside.

Trim leeks of all green parts, root bases, and any tough outer leaves. Wash them several times in cold water. Cut lengthwise, into the center but not through the leeks. Holding leeks together, rinse them under cold running water to make sure that all grit is washed away. Open the leeks to butterflies and place in a steamer basket over boiling water. Cover and steam for 10 to 12 minutes, or until tender. Remove to paper towels and drain well. Set aside.

Combine gelatin with 1 cup of stock in a small saucepan and allow to sit for 2 minutes to soften. Then place the pan over low heat and stir for about 1 minute, or until gelatin has dissolved. Heat the remaining 3 cups of stock in a medium saucepan over medium heat until just warmed. Whisk in softened gelatin, stirring until blended. Season to taste with salt and pepper and let cool to room temperature. When cool, stir in the herbs. Place about 2 tablespoons of the herbed aspic in a very small container in an ice bath for a few minutes, then test for consistency and seasoning: It should be meltingly soft yet firm, but not thick like Jell-O.

Spray a 12 × 4 × 4-inch terrine with nonstick vegetable spray. Carefully line it with plastic film, allowing a 2- to 3-inch overhang all around. Pour ¼ cup of aspic into the bottom.

Pour 1 cup of aspic into a bowl to use for dipping the vegetables. One at a time, dip eggplant slices into the aspic. Fit two slices into the bottom of the terrine to cover it. Lay four slices, slightly overlapping, on each long side, allowing them to cover the sides and to overhang the edge by about 2 inches. Pour in aspic to cover and season to taste with salt and pepper. Next, add a layer of yellow squash, followed by a layer of zucchini, dipping each slice in aspic and seasoning as you layer. Follow with a layer of mushrooms (trimming to fit, if necessary), dipping in aspic as you layer. Push vegetables down and add aspic as needed to keep top layer covered with aspic.

Gently pull leeks apart, being careful not to tear the segments. Dip each piece into the aspic, and place a double layer of leeks on top of the mushrooms. Push down, season, and add aspic, if necessary, to cover.

Dip the artichoke bottoms into the aspic. Press them down into the leek layer, seasoning and adding aspic to cover if necessary. Add another double layer of leeks, pushing down, seasoning, and adding aspic as required.

Dipping each piece in aspic as you go, place a layer of alternating red and yellow pepper pieces, then repeat with another layer. Push down, season, and add aspic as needed.

Finally, gently push down on vegetables to force out any air pockets and to ensure that aspic covers all the vegetables and fills any holes. Fold eggplant up and over the top, seasoning and adding aspic to cover if necessary. Fold the plastic film over to cover tightly. Cut a small vent in the top and give a final push to expel air. Place in the refrigerator for 8 hours to allow flavors to blend and aspic to set. When ready to serve, lift from the terrine by holding onto the plastic film. Unwrap. Place on a cutting board and slice, crosswise, into ½-inch-thick slices, using a serrated knife.

SUGGESTED WINE: This needs a complex wine, possibly a Meritage, such as Langtry Vineyard by Guenoc.

Slow-Roasted
Beet and Goat Cheese Gâteau

Serves 6

A simple and visually appealing appetizer that is particularly colorful, with the deep red of the beets and creamy white of the goat cheese surrounded by the bright greens and mellow brown walnuts. It is important that the beets be of similar size. I like the discs to be no more than 1½ to 2 inches in diameter—any larger and the layers look unwieldy; any smaller and the presentation looks skimpy.

14 medium beets (see Note)
Approximately 4 cups coarse salt
1 cup Sherry-Shallot Vinaigrette (page 193)
2 cups mizuna (see Note)
1 pound soft goat cheese
1 cup toasted walnut pieces

Preheat oven to 300°F.

Trim off beet greens, leaving about 1 inch of stem. Scrub well and pat dry.

Place a ½-inch layer of salt over the surface of a baking sheet with sides. Position beets, root ends down, in the salt. Place in preheated oven and roast for about 90 minutes, or until tender. Remove beets from salt. Place them in a bowl and cover with plastic film. Set aside until cool enough to handle.

Lower oven temperature to 150°F.

When beets are cool enough to handle, slip off skins. Trim ends to flat surfaces. Slice each beet, crosswise, into ¼-inch discs. Re-form each beet to its whole shape and set aside individually. Finely chop the beet scraps and whisk into the vinaigrette. Taste and adjust the seasoning if necessary. Set aside.

Wash and dry mizuna. Set aside.

Put goat cheese in a pastry bag fitted with a star tip. Lay pastry bag on a baking sheet in preheated oven. Turn oven off and let the goat cheese rest for about 2 minutes, or until softened and warm. Remove from oven.

Working with the first beet, pipe a layer of goat cheese onto one beet disc. Top with another beet disc, then pipe on another layer of goat cheese. Top with a final beet disc to make 3 beet and 2 cheese layers. Repeat with the remaining beets.

Place 2 beet gâteaus in the center of each of 6 serving plates. Sprinkle equal portions of greens and walnuts around the outer edges of the plates. Drizzle with vinaigrette and serve immediately.

SUGGESTED WINE: A clean and simple Pinot Blanc from Alsace

A NOTE FROM JUDIE

This recipe is easy to prepare. It looks like a million dollars and it combines two of my favorite tastes. At Aureole, the plate is further garnished with candied orange peel—delicious, but truly an unnecessary extra for the home cook. We have asked that you cook 14 beets to allow for any breakage—an unlikely occurrence, but leftover beets are great in a salad or quickly sautéed. Leaving a bit of stem on the beets keeps them from bleeding off much of their color when cooking.

Charlie uses mizuna, which is a delicate, peppery salad green. However, you can use any delicate, tasty green, such as watercress, if mizuna is not available.

Roasted Asparagus
with Parma Ham and
Roasted Pepper Coulis

Serves 6

This beautiful appetizer is a terrific boon when entertaining, as so much can be done ahead of time. The puree can be made and placed on the plates (wrapped in plastic film) early in the day. The asparagus bundles can be put together and then baked just before serving. Try to purchase asparagus spears of uniform shape so that the finished presentation is as attractive as possible.

2 red bell peppers
5 tablespoons plus 1 teaspoon olive oil
1 tablespoon white wine vinegar
Coarse salt
Pepper
36 medium spears asparagus
6 thin slices Parma ham (or prosciutto)
4 sheets prepared filo dough (see Note)
¾ cup melted unsalted butter
6 tablespoons dry bread crumbs
1 cup baby arugula leaves

Preheat oven to 375°F.

Rub peppers with 2 tablespoons of olive oil. Place them on a baking sheet in preheated oven and roast for about 25 minutes, or until they're almost charred. Remove from oven and place in a plastic container with a lid or a plastic bag with a tie to steam and cool. When cool enough to handle, push off skins and remove stems and seeds. Place peppers in a food processor fitted with the metal blade and puree along with the vinegar, 1 tablespoon of olive oil, and 3 tablespoons of water. Season to taste with salt and pepper. Scrape the mixture from the processor bowl and set it aside.

Wash asparagus and, using a sharp knife, trim bottoms to make spears of equal length. Place the asparagus in boiling water for 1 minute. Drain and refresh under cold running water and pat dry with paper towels. Place in a bowl and carefully toss with 2 tablespoons of olive oil.

Cut the ham in half lengthwise. Hold 3 asparagus spears together. Wrap one strip of ham around the center of the asparagus bundle and set aside. Continue making bundles until you have 12.

Thaw and handle filo dough as directed on package. Carefully lay 1 sheet of filo dough out onto a damp towel. Lightly brush it with some of the melted butter and sprinkle it with 3 tablespoons bread crumbs. Butter another sheet and place on top of the crumbed sheet. Using a very sharp knife, carefully cut the filo sheets, from top to bottom, into 6 strips. Roll one filo strip around the center of an asparagus-ham bundle. Continue until you have prepared 6 bundles. Repeat the process with the remaining filo sheets, butter, crumbs, and 6 remaining asparagus bundles.

Place bundles on a baking sheet and then into the preheated oven. Bake for 9 to 12 minutes, or until the pastry is golden brown. Remove from the oven.

Toss the arugula leaves with the remaining teaspoon of oil. Set aside.

Place a pool of pepper puree in the center of each of 6 plates. Cross 2 asparagus bundles over the puree. Garnish with a few arugula leaves and serve immediately.

SUGGESTED WINE: Something complex, such as a white Châteauneuf-du-Pape or Coudelet de Beaucastel

A NOTE FROM JUDIE

Prepared filo dough is available in the refrigerator section of most supermarkets and specialty-food stores or from one of the sources listed at the back of this book. Be sure to follow the manufacturer's directions for handling. How grateful home cooks should be for this convenience—I can't imagine carefully stretching and pulling the dough for this tissue paper-thin pastry.

Foie Gras Terrine

Makes one 12-inch terrine

Although very expensive. the taste. matched with its ease of preparation. makes a foie gras terrine the home cook's dinner-party scene stealer. It is not for an everyday meal but is a worthwhile extravagance whenever celebration is called for.

2 raw foie gras (see Note)
½ cup white port
2 teaspoons coarse salt
2 teaspoons sugar
½ teaspoon freshly ground white pepper

Remove the foie gras from the refrigerator. place them on a cutting board covered with plastic film. and allow them to warm slightly. Carefully divide each foie gras into its two lobes. Using a small. very sharp knife, split open one lobe. Begin carefully pushing the liver to open it further. removing the veins as you go. Do not cut through outer skin. Try to locate the main vein stem and pull it up and out to release the smaller veins and arteries. Keep spreading the liver to locate and remove the veins. During the process. the liver will begin to look like paste. The vein removal requires patience and vigilance. Proceed in the same manner with the remaining lobes.

When all veins are removed. sprinkle foie gras with port. Lightly wrap in plastic film and refrigerate for 1 hour.

Combine salt. sugar. and pepper and set aside.

Preheat oven to 225°F.

Remove foie gras from refrigerator. Gently pat a 1½-inch layer of foie gras into the bottom of a 12 × 4 × 4-inch porcelain terrine. Sprinkle with seasoning mix. Cover with plastic film and tamp down with the palm of your hand. Remove plastic and continue making layers of foie gras and seasoning. covering with plastic film and tamping down as you go. until you have used all of the foie gras. Smooth the top and then tightly wrap the entire dish in plastic film. Fold a terry hand towel into the shape of the terrine. Place the towel in a pan at least 5 inches deep and large enough to hold the filled terrine. Set the filled terrine on the towel and fill the pan with enough cold water to come up almost to the top of the terrine. Carefully place the pan in preheated oven and bake for 20 minutes. Remove from oven and lift the terrine from the water bath. Unwrap and allow to cool on a wire rack. When cool. cover with a piece of parchment paper and refrigerate for at least 8 hours.

To unmold. wrap terrine with a hot towel and turn it out onto a well-chilled serving platter. Cut it into ⅛-inch-thick slices and serve with crisp toast.

SUGGESTED WINE: A late-harvest Riesling. such as Navarro or Joseph Phelps from California

A NOTE FROM JUDIE

Once available only in France, and most particularly in Perigord, Alsace, and Gascony, fresh foie gras is now produced and shipped, overnight, to any place in the United States by D'Artagnan, a marvelously innovative company based in New Jersey. This American foie gras has been developed using moulard ducks raised in perpetual soft light, which encourages them to overeat. Although the liver is the most luxurious part of the ducks, the breasts and legs are equally useful.

Terrines and mousses can be made from the less-expensive, smaller, grainier, grade "B" liver. Remember to use a very sharp knife when removing the veins from the liver. (Don't use the knife to cut but only to locate the veins and lift them out.)

Foie Gras Mousse

Makes 1 pound

How could something so luxurious be so easy to make? This is a perfect party hors d'oeuvre, since it can be prepared well in advance.

5 shallots
1 teaspoon olive oil
1 cup Madeira wine
½ pound fresh foie gras (see Note)
½ pound (2 sticks) unsalted butter at room temperature
Coarse salt
Freshly ground white pepper
Toast points

Peel and finely mince shallots. Heat olive oil in a small sauté pan over medium heat. Add shallots and sauté for about 4 minutes, or until shallots are translucent and have sweated off most of their liquid. Remove from the heat and allow to cool.

Place Madeira in a very small saucepan over medium-low heat. Simmer for about 15 minutes, or until reduced by half, taking care that the alcohol does not flame. Remove from heat and let cool.

Cut foie gras into small pieces. Place a small nonstick sauté pan over high heat. When very hot, add foie gras. Sauté for 1 minute. Remove from heat and let cool for 5 minutes.

Place cooked foie gras in a food processor fitted with the metal blade. Add shallots and process, using quick on-and-off turns, until mixture is almost smooth. With the motor running, add the butter and Madeira, a bit at a time. Process until the butter is well incorporated and the mixture is smooth. Taste and adjust the seasoning with salt and pepper. Scrape the mixture from the processor into a small decorative mold or terrine. Cover with plastic film and refrigerate for 3 hours, or until well chilled.

Serve well chilled with toast points (see photograph on page 4).

If you want to unmold the mousse, first line the mold (or terrine) with plastic film, leaving at least a 3-inch overhang. When it is well chilled, lift the mousse out of the mold by pulling up the plastic film overhang. After you have unmolded the mousse and placed it on an attractive serving plate, you may garnish it with fresh lobster or crab, Herb-Potato Maximes (page 192), carrot discs, chopped chives, or whatever you like.

You can also use a pastry bag fitted with the star tip to pipe the mousse directly on crackers or toast points. Or, you can form the mousse into quenelle shapes by molding it between two wet tablespoons.

A NOTE FROM JUDIE

You can also make this mousse using canned, imported foie gras. If so, do not sauté it before processing with the shallots. It won't be quite as delicious, but it will still be a winning first course or hors d'oeuvre.

Sautéed Escalopes of Foie Gras with Savory Corn Cakes

Serves 6

If the raw foie gras is very cold and the pan is very hot, this sauté will be superb. Use your judgment when reducing the sauce—it should just reach a coating consistency. I like the corn cake under the foie gras for two reasons: It adds a wonderful contrast to the smooth texture of the liver, and it also absorbs the rich juices that seep from the warm liver and mingle with the slightly acidic sauce. I believe that hot foie gras, whether sautéed or roasted, always requires a taste of acid as a foil for its richness. In this case, I use vinegar, but at other times I use citrus fruits, wine reductions, or even something as forceful as rhubarb.

> 1 foie gras (see page 14)
> ¼ pound mesclun, rocket, or other tender baby greens
> 6 Savory Corn Cakes (recipe follows)
> Coarse salt
> Freshly ground black pepper
> 3 tablespoons red wine vinegar
> ½ cup rich Chicken Stock (see Note, page 189)
> 2 tablespoons unsalted butter
> 1 tablespoon minced fresh parsley
> ½ tablespoon minced fresh chives

Separate the foie gras lobes by cutting the connecting tendon with a very sharp knife. For six people, you will only need the larger lobe, so reserve the remaining lobe for a pâté or mousse. Carefully remove all veins but do not smash liver. Pat it dry. Place lobe flat on a cool, clean surface and, using a sharp knife dipped into very hot water, cut, at a slight angle, to make a ⅝- to ¾-inch-thick slice of foie gras weighing about 3 ounces. Continue cutting until you have 6 pieces of equal size, dipping the knife into very hot water each time you slice. Lay pieces flat and, with the tip of the knife, cut a crosshatch design ⅛ inch deep across the top of each piece. Cover and refrigerate until ready to sear.

Preheat oven to 275°F.

Wash and carefully dry greens. Place equal portions at the top of each of 6 luncheon-size plates.

Place the corn cakes on a small sheet pan. Place in preheated oven to warm through.

Place a 10-inch nonstick sauté pan over high heat. Do not oil pan! Remove foie gras from refrigerator. Season both sides with salt and pepper. When the pan is very hot, add the foie gras, scored side down. Using your fingertips, gently push slices into pan, so that foie gras immediately begins to render its fat. Cook for about 2 minutes,

A NOTE FROM JUDIE

Like all home cooks, I've been more than a bit intimidated by foie gras: It's so expensive and what if I ruin it? Charlie's simple sauté works every time. I think it is that initial push down with the fingertips that gives the extra crisp touch to this perfect appetizer. On the restaurant stove, the heat is awesome and the chef has to watch that the liver doesn't burn. You should too!

or until bottom begins to caramelize and quite a bit of fat has been exuded. Turn and brown the other side for 2 minutes, or until well crisped. Remove cooked foie gras to a warm plate and keep warm.

Drain off half of the fat and return pan to high heat. Add the vinegar, stirring to release any browned bits from pan. Add stock. Cook, stirring constantly, for about 3 minutes, or until liquid is reduced by half and sauce coats the back of a spoon.

Whisk in the butter and herbs, stirring until smooth and well incorporated. Return foie gras to pan. Carefully spoon sauce over foie gras slices. Remove from heat.

Immediately place a warm corn cake in the center of each prepared plate. Lay a slice of foie gras on top and spoon a bit of sauce over the top and around the plate.

Serve immediately.

Savory Corn Cakes

Makes about 12

1 cup all-purpose flour
½ cup cornmeal
½ tablespoon baking powder
½ teaspoon coarse salt
2 tablespoons unsalted butter
¼ cup sugar
1 large egg
½ tablespoon pure maple syrup
½ tablespoon honey
1 cup milk

Preheat oven to 350°F.

Combine flour, cornmeal, baking powder, and salt. Set aside.

Beat butter and sugar together until well blended. Beat in egg, maple syrup, and honey. Add dry ingredients alternately with the milk until all ingredients have been added and mixture is well blended.

Spray twelve 4-inch round by ¾-inch deep (nonstick, if possible) molds with nonstick vegetable spray. Fill with equal portions of cornmeal batter. Place in preheated oven and bake for 12 minutes, or until edges pull away from the sides and centers are set. Remove from oven and serve warm. Or, allow to cool on a wire rack. Then, when ready to serve, reheat in a preheated 275°F oven for about 5 minutes, or until warmed through.

SUGGESTED WINE: A fine-quality Sauternes

Lobster Cocktail with Light Lemon Sabayon

Serves 6

A *sabayon* is a light, foamy dessert sauce made with egg yolks, wine, and sugar. Here I've used the term for a light, refreshing mayonnaise sauce.

2 tablespoons white wine vinegar
four 1½-pound lobsters
½ cup crème fraîche, chilled
¼ cup mayonnaise
2 tablespoons fresh lemon juice
Zest of one lemon
Coarse salt
Pepper
1 cup tiny arugula leaves
6 tablespoons Citrus Vinaigrette (page 193)
6 corn madeleines (optional; see Note)

Place 7½ gallons of water and vinegar in a deep stockpot over high heat. Bring to a boil. Carefully add lobsters to the boiling water. Cover and boil for exactly 5 minutes. Drain well and set aside to cool.

Place chilled crème fraîche in a small, chilled bowl. Using a hand mixer, beat for about 3 minutes, or until whipped and airy.

Whisk together the mayonnaise, lemon juice, zest, and salt and pepper to taste in a nonreactive bowl. Carefully fold in the crème fraîche so as not to lose volume. Cover and refrigerate.

Wash greens and pat dry. Wrap in a damp paper towel and refrigerate.

When lobsters are cool, twist the tail of each free from the rest of the body. Using kitchen shears, carefully cut the underside of the tail shell and gently pry the shell open. Remove the meat, keeping the piece whole. Using the back edge of a knife, crack the claws and carefully remove shell and lift out meat, keeping it whole. Crack the knuckles and remove the meat. Cut twelve even crosswise slices from the tails. Set aside. Cut all scraps and remaining claws and knuckle meat into ½-inch dice. Place in a nonreactive bowl. Remove *sabayon* from the refrigerator and fold into the diced lobster.

Divide the lobster mixture into 6 equal portions. Place in 6 chilled champagne saucers (or other shallow glass bowls). Top each with two lobster slices. Garnish with a few sprigs of arugula. Drizzle lightly with citrus vinaigrette. Serve immediately, with warm corn madeleines, if desired.

SUGGESTED WINE: A blanc de blancs sparkling wine, such as Iron Horse

Sea Scallop Sandwiches with Citrus Juices

Serves 6

There are a few crucial steps that will ensure that this very simple dish becomes spectacular: The potatoes must be in long strands and be squeezed absolutely dry; you must work quickly so that the sandwiches can be served almost immediately after frying, while they are still very hot and crisp; and the herbs should be added to the sauce just before serving so that they retain their bright green color and heady aromas.

1 cup Chicken Stock (page 189)
12 large, fresh sea scallops
4 large baking potatoes, peeled, washed, and well dried
2 tablespoons superfine flour (such as Wondra)
Coarse salt
Freshly ground white pepper
¼ cup fresh lemon juice
¼ cup fresh orange juice
2 cups safflower (or other vegetable) oil (see A Note from Charlie)
3 tablespoons unsalted butter
1 tablespoon chopped fresh chervil
1 tablespoon chopped fresh chives

Line a sheet pan with parchment paper. Set aside.

Place stock in a small saucepan over medium-high heat. Bring to a boil. Continue boiling for about 5 minutes, or until reduced to ⅛ cup. Set aside.

Slice each scallop, crosswise, then into ½-inch discs. Pat dry.

Shred potatoes, lengthwise, on a mandoline or other vegetable slicer set to a very fine thickness. Place in a clean, thick, cotton kitchen towel. Pull up corners of towel and tightly squeeze until all the water has been pulled from the potatoes. Fluff up the potatoes and divide them in half. Use one half to make twelve small mounds on the prepared sheet pan. Dust each mound with a bit of the flour.

Slightly overlap 2 scallop discs on top of each mound. Season liberally with salt and pepper.

Use the remaining potatoes to cover each of the scallop-covered mounds evenly. Season lightly with salt and pepper. Dust each sandwich with remaining flour. Do not press layers down.

Line a sheet pan with double layers of paper towel. Set aside.

Strain citrus juices through a fine sieve. Set aside.

This is Charlie's signature dish, and by now it seems simple to him. To see him standing on the kitchen line at the height of a Saturday-night rush, commandeering the mandoline and furiously shredding potatoes, is to see a man in love with his job! I've tried these at home on my less-than-hot home stove—they are almost as good as Charlie's, but they do take a bit longer to crisp. I also found that a food processor does not shred potatoes into long enough strands to hold the sandwiches together. However, these are so delicious, I know you'll want to invest in a mandoline to make them perfectly. Charlie always serves 2 of these per person, but one is more than enough for me. I would use 2 for a main course at a special luncheon.

Preheat oven to 275°F.

Place 1 cup of oil in each of two 10- to 12-inch nonstick sauté pans. Place pans over medium-high heat and heat for about 2 minutes, or until oil is almost smoking. Using a spatula, carefully place 4 sandwiches in each pan, making sure that they hold their shapes. Lower heat slightly and cook for approximately 5 minutes, or until bottoms are golden-brown and crisp. Carefully turn and brown the other sides. When well browned and crisp, remove from pans onto lined sheet pan to drain. When well drained, lay out, singly, on unlined sheet pan and place in preheated oven, with door open, to keep warm while preparing sauce.

Add citrus juices to reduced chicken stock. Place over medium-high heat and bring to a boil. Continue boiling for about 4 minutes, or until sauce coats the back of a spoon. Whisk in butter, a bit at a time, until well incorporated and smooth. Check seasoning. Add salt and pepper, if necessary. Stir in herbs.

Spoon an equal portion of sauce onto each of 6 warm serving plates, making a circle in the center of the plate. Lean 2 sandwiches up against each other in the center of the sauce. Serve immediately.

SUGGESTED WINE: A Fumé Blanc, such as Robert Mondavi

Crab Lasagna with Tomato-Basil Coulis

Serves 6

This is an unusual way to serve crab, but it is light, refreshing, and one of my favorite seafood dishes. It can also be served as a main course for a summer's lunch. Simply serve slightly larger portions, and add a loaf of crusty French bread and a glass or two of chilled white wine or a frosty pitcher of beer.

½ cup celery in ¼-inch dice
½ cup carrot in ¼-inch dice
¼ cup red onion in ¼-inch dice
1 pound fresh jumbo lump crabmeat (see A Note from Both of Us)
2 tablespoons fresh lemon juice
⅔ cup mayonnaise
2 tablespoons chopped fresh parsley
Coarse salt
Freshly ground white pepper
1 tablespoon olive oil
4 rectangular sheets fresh Semolina Pasta, at least 8 × 4 inches (page 191)
6 to 8 romaine lettuce leaves
1 recipe Tomato-Basil Coulis (recipe follows)
6 fresh basil sprigs

A NOTE FROM JUDIE

This recipe is so easy to do that you might want to make the pasta from scratch. However, you can also buy ready-made "fresh" pasta sheets or even dried lasagne noodles, which you could trim to fit.

Cook each type of diced vegetable separately in a saucepan of rapidly boiling salted water for 3 minutes, or until crisp-tender. Remove from water and refresh under cold running water. Place in a clean, dry kitchen towel and twist to squeeze out all liquid. Set aside.

Pick through the crabmeat, discarding any shell or cartilage pieces. Place cleaned crab in a mixing bowl along with the diced vegetables. Sprinkle lemon juice over all and toss to combine. Fold in the mayonnaise and parsley, mixing thoroughly but taking care not to pack the mixture together. Season to taste. Cover and refrigerate.

Line an 8 × 4 × 3½-inch terrine or mold with plastic film, leaving at least a 2-inch overhang all around. Using your fingers, coat the interior of the lined terrine with the olive oil. Set aside.

Bring a large pot of salted water to a boil over high heat. Cut the pasta sheets into 4 strips the exact size of the terrine (see A Note from Judie). One at a time, drop pasta strips into boiling water and cook for 1 minute, or until just al dente. Remove from water and drain thoroughly. Lay one strip on the bottom of the prepared terrine. Separately, lay remaining strips out on paper towels. While water is boiling, blanch romaine leaves for 5 seconds, or until just wilted. Remove them from the water and refresh under cold running water. Pat dry.

(continued)

Remove crab mixture from the refrigerator and divide it into 3 equal portions.

Place a layer of romaine on top of the pasta in the terrine. Using one portion, spread a layer of the crab mixture over the romaine. Continue making layers in the same sequence until you have used the three portions of crab, ending with a layer of pasta. Fold the plastic film up and over the top of the terrine. Tightly wrap the entire terrine with plastic film. Place another heavy terrine or pan on top to weight the layers down. Refrigerate for at least 4 hours, or up to 8 hours (until well chilled).

When well chilled, remove terrine from the refrigerator and unwrap. Invert onto a cutting board and remove all the plastic film.

Ladle a small portion of the *coulis* into the center of each of 6 chilled plates. Turn the plates to spread the *coulis* out over the bottoms. Using a very sharp knife, carefully cut the terrine into twelve ½-inch slices (reserving the remainder for a late-night snack!). Overlap 2 slices in the center of each plate. Garnish with a basil sprig and serve immediately.

Tomato-Basil Coulis

Makes about 1½ cups

2 large, very ripe tomatoes
1 shallot
1 tablespoon olive oil
1 tablespoon red wine vinegar
3 tablespoons minced fresh basil
Coarse salt
Pepper

Wash the tomatoes and pat dry. Cut in half, lengthwise, and remove cores. Cut each half into quarters and set aside.

Peel and finely mince shallot.

Heat oil in a small saucepan over medium heat. Add the shallot and sauté for 1 minute. Add the tomato and sauté for 5 minutes. Stir in vinegar. Scrape into a blender and puree. Strain through a fine sieve into a nonreactive container. Stir in basil and season to taste with salt and pepper. Cover and refrigerate until ready to use.

SUGGESTED WINE: A Sancerre, a perfect example being a '92 by Lucien Crochet

Pepper-Seared
Salmon and New Potato
Terrine with Spring Leeks

Makes one 12-inch terrine

This is a beautiful terrine. Pale colors combine with delicate flavors here to make a light first course. With little fat, the aromatic, almost sweet vegetables and rich fish create gossamer layers that delight the palate. All this and it is relatively easy to put together!

15 medium-sized new potatoes
6 cups Chicken Stock (page 189)
4 cloves garlic, peeled
4 sprigs fresh thyme
2 bay leaves
Coarse salt
Pepper
3 medium leeks
2 ½ pounds skinless, boneless, center-cut salmon fillet (see A Note from Charlie)
2 tablespoons olive oil
2 tablespoons unflavored gelatin
1 tablespoon minced fresh parsley

Peel potatoes. Place in a large saucepan over medium heat with 4 cups of stock, 2 cloves garlic, 2 sprigs thyme, 1 bay leaf, and salt and pepper to taste. Bring to a boil. Lower heat and simmer for 15 minutes, or until the potatoes are tender. Drain, reserving liquid. Discard garlic, thyme, and bay leaf. Set potatoes and liquid aside, separately.

Trim leeks of all green stalks and root ends. Wash them well. Using a sharp knife, cut them lengthwise down the centers. Separate leeks, one leaf at a time. Place them in cold water to remove all traces of grit. Pat dry.

Place leeks in a large saucepan over medium heat with remaining stock, garlic, thyme, bay leaf, and salt and pepper to taste. Cook for about 4 minutes, or until leeks are tender. Drain, reserving liquid. Discard garlic, thyme, and bay leaf. Set leeks and liquid aside, separately.

Slice salmon in pieces ¾ inch thick by 2 inches wide. You will need enough to cover the length of the terrine three times. Reserve any remaining fish for another use. Season to taste with salt and pepper. Place olive oil in a medium-sized, nonstick sauté pan over medium-high heat. When very hot, add salmon and sear for 1 minute. Sear other side and remove from pan. You want the fish to remain almost raw. Quickly drain on a paper towel and place in the refrigerator to stop cooking.

(continued)

A NOTE FROM CHARLIE

You could use other firm-fleshed, succulent fish for this terrine, but nothing will give the perfect pink layers that the salmon will.

Combine reserved cooking liquids from the potatoes and leeks in a medium saucepan over high heat. Bring to a boil. Lower heat and simmer for about 10 minutes, or until reduced to 4 cups. Taste and adjust seasoning with salt and pepper. Reserve and keep warm.

Place gelatin in a small saucepan with ½ cup of the reduced cooking liquid and let sit for 2 minutes to soften. Then place over low heat and stir for about 1 minute, or until gelatin has dissolved. Stir into reserved liquid. Stir in parsley. Cover and keep warm.

Cut potatoes into very thin (less than ⅛ inch thick) slices. Place in a bowl and add about ½ cup of aspic to just moisten.

Carefully line a 12 × 4 × 4-inch ceramic terrine with plastic film, allowing a 2- to 3-inch overhang all around. Pour just enough aspic into the bottom to cover.

Pour 1 cup of the aspic into a small bowl. One at a time, dip leek pieces into the aspic in the bowl. Cover the bottom and line the sides of the terrine with a single layer of leeks, leaving a 2-inch overhang around the edges. Place a layer of potato on the bottom of the terrine.

Cut one salmon piece, lengthwise, into thirds. Place a layer of salmon on top of the potatoes, using 2⅓ pieces.

Pour in about ¼ cup of aspic and press down to cover the salmon with aspic. Using the same amount, make another layer of potatoes and salmon. Add ¼ cup of aspic and press down. Again layer potatoes, then salmon, then aspic, and press down.

Make a final layer of potatoes and cover with aspic, pressing down to cover well. Place a layer of leeks on top of the potatoes. Fold leek overhang up and over. Add aspic and press down to force out any air pockets and to ensure that aspic covers the potatoes and salmon and fills any holes.

Fold the plastic film over to cover tightly. Place in the refrigerator for at least 8 hours. When ready to serve, lift from the terrine by holding onto the plastic film. Unwrap. Place on a cutting board and slice, crosswise, using a serrated knife, into ½-inch-thick slices.

SUGGESTED WINE: A Chardonnay such as a '93 Talbot

Warm New Potato Blinis with Seared Salmon, Cultured Cream, and Osetra Caviar

Serves 6

Blinis are the traditional Russian backdrop for caviar and smoked salmon. They are usually made from buckwheat flour and are yeast-raised, but I love this much simpler potato version. Simple but still a terrific background for salmon and caviar.

1 ½ pounds salmon fillet
1 pound new potatoes
¼ cup milk
4 tablespoons all-purpose flour
3 large eggs
3 large egg whites
Coarse salt
Freshly ground white pepper
3 tablespoons grapeseed oil
⅔ cup crème fraîche
3 ounces Osetra caviar (see Note)
3 tablespoons minced chives
Six 4-inch chive pieces, end points only

Line two baking sheets with parchment paper. Set aside.

Cut salmon fillet, crosswise, into eighteen 1-ounce medallions (see A Note from Judie). Pat dry. Cover and refrigerate. Reserve remaining pieces for another use.

Peel potatoes and cut into quarters. Place in a medium saucepan with salted water to cover over medium-high heat. Bring to a boil. Lower heat and simmer for 10 minutes, or until tender. Drain well. Place in a ricer and push into a mixing bowl. Stir in milk, then slowly beat in flour. When everything is well incorporated, beat in the whole eggs.

Beat egg whites until soft peaks form. Fold them into the potato batter. Season to taste with salt and pepper.

Preheat oven to 175°F.

Place a drop of oil on a medium nonstick griddle. When hot, ladle batter to make blinis about 2 inches in diameter. Cook, turning once, for 1½ minutes per side, or until golden. Continue making blinis until you have 18, keeping cooked blinis warm on one of the prepared parchment-lined baking sheets in the preheated oven.

Remove the salmon medallions from the refrigerator. Lay them out, singly, and lightly season with salt and pepper on one side only. Add a few drops of oil to 2 non-stick pans over high heat. When very hot, place the salmon medallions, seasoned sides down, in the pans. Sear for 1 minute. Remove to the other prepared baking sheet and place in preheated oven.

Starting at 12 o'clock, place alternating layers of blinis and salmon down the middle of each of 6 warm plates, beginning with a blini and ending with salmon. With a fork, lightly mix the crème fraîche to loosen it slightly. Drizzle 2 table-spoonsful down the center of each blini-salmon combination. Place a spoonful of caviar in the center. Sprinkle the chives over all. Set a chive point between a layer of blini and salmon. Serve immediately.

SUGGESTED WINE: Champagne; something yeasty, such as a Louis Roederer Brut

Pepper-Seared Haddock and "Brandade" Cake with Warm Black Truffle Vinaigrette

Serves 6

*B*randade de morue is a traditional Provençal dish made with a pounded mixture of salt cod, olive oil, garlic, and cream, served with thick slices of toast, and garnished with black-truffle shavings. This is my easy-to-make version of one of France's great peasant dishes.

3 bunches mâche (or other soft baby greens or lettuces; see A Note from Judie)
1 ½ pounds boneless haddock (see A Note from Charlie)
Coarse salt
2 medium Idaho potatoes
8 small new potatoes
2 teaspoons minced garlic
4 cloves Roasted Garlic (page 197)
1 tablespoon minced fresh parsley
¼ teaspoon cayenne pepper
¼ teaspoon freshly ground black pepper
1 cup superfine flour (such as Wondra)
2 large eggs
1 ½ cups fine bread crumbs
1 cup Truffle Vinaigrette (page 194; see A Note from Charlie)
5 tablespoons canola or other unflavored oil

Wash mâche and pat it dry. Wrap in damp paper towels and refrigerate until ready to serve.

Preheat oven to 350°F.

Cut haddock into six 2-ounce blocks, reserving all scraps. Set aside.

Season haddock scraps to taste with salt. Lightly wrap them in aluminum foil and place on a baking sheet in preheated oven. Bake for 10 minutes, or until just cooked and flaky. Remove from oven. Unwrap and let cool. Pat dry.

Peel potatoes. Separately, cut each type into 1-inch pieces and place each in a saucepan with water to cover, 1 teaspoon of minced garlic, and salt to taste. Bring both pans to a boil over high heat. Lower heat and simmer for 15 minutes, or until tender. Drain well. Push Idaho potatoes through a ricer into a mixing bowl. Chop the new potatoes and add them to the Idaho potatoes. Flake fish scraps into the potatoes and stir to combine.

Push roasted garlic from its skin. Combine it with parsley, and stir into potato mixture along with cayenne, salt to taste, and black pepper.

Place half of the flour on a clean, flat surface. Place a 2½-inch ring mold on the flour. Fit some potato mixture into the ring. Sprinkle some flour on top and lift the ring up. Continue making cakes until you have 6.

Whisk the eggs in a shallow bowl. Place bread crumbs in another shallow bowl. Dip fish cakes, one at a time, into the egg wash and then into the bread crumbs. Gently tap to release any excess crumbs.

Place truffle vinaigrette in a small saucepan over very low heat for about 2 minutes, or until just warm. Remove from heat and keep warm.

Heat 3 tablespoons of oil in a heavy, nonstick sauté pan over medium heat. Add fish cakes and fry, turning once, for about 4 minutes, or until golden and heated through. Set aside; cover and keep warm.

Heat the remaining oil in a large, nonstick sauté pan over medium-high heat. Season the fish blocks with salt and pepper. Place them in hot pan and cook, turning once, for 4 minutes, or until just seared.

Place equal portions of mâche on each of 6 plates. Place a hot fish cake in the center. Place a piece of fish on top.

Drizzle with warm vinaigrette and serve immediately.

SUGGESTED WINE: A well-balanced Chardonnay

Sesame-Seared Tuna Cake with Mustard Vinaigrette

Serves 6

Almost raw, this warm, barely cooked tuna cake, coated with crispy sesame seeds, laps up the vinaigrette. The rich fish absolutely shines against the spicy, acidic flavors, while the sweet mesclun offers balance to the plate.

6 cups mesclun (or other tender, young lettuces or greens)
8 medium new potatoes
1 tablespoon coarse salt plus more to taste
1½ pounds tuna fillet, trimmed of all fat and skin
2 tablespoons extra-virgin olive oil
½ teaspoon cayenne pepper
5 tablespoons canola oil
2 cups toasted sesame seeds
1 cup Mustard Vinaigrette (page 194)
1 cup Parsnip Chips (optional; pages 192–193)

Wash mesclun and pat or spin dry. Wrap in damp paper towels and refrigerate until ready to use.

Place potatoes in a medium saucepan and add water to cover and salt to taste. Place over high heat and bring to a boil. Lower heat and simmer for 20 minutes, or until tender. Drain well. Allow the potatoes to rest until cool enough to handle. Peel and slice, crosswise, into ¼-inch-thick discs. Set aside.

Finely chop tuna. Combine it with olive oil, 1 tablespoon salt, and cayenne. Divide into 6 equal portions. Form each portion into an even-sided cake about 2½ inches in diameter.

Heat 2 tablespoons of canola oil in a medium sauté pan over medium-high heat. Add potatoes and cook, turning frequently, until lightly browned and slightly crisp. Remove from pan and drain on paper towels.

Place sesame seeds in a shallow bowl. One at a time, roll tuna cakes in sesame seeds until well covered. Heat remaining 3 tablespoons of canola oil in a heavy, nonstick sauté pan over medium-high heat. Add tuna cakes and fry, turning once, for 1½ minutes per side, or until golden. Drain on paper towels.

Remove mesclun from the refrigerator and place equal portions in the center of each of 6 plates. Place an equal portion of potato discs in a circle in the center of the mesclun. Place a hot tuna cake on top of the potato circle. Drizzle mustard vinaigrette over all. Top with parsnip chips, if desired. Serve immediately.

SUGGESTED WINE: A floral, fruity white wine, such as La Jota Viognier

A NOTE FROM JUDIE

Charlie prefers to fry the tuna cakes in clarified butter, as he thinks the flavor adds even more richness to this dish. However, we suggest canola oil to keep saturated fat content down. If you really want the taste of Charlie's preparation, however, use clarified butter.

I think that the parsnip-chip garnish really completes this dish. I have made the chips the day before service and stored them at room temperature, tightly covered. They were delicious!

Try this with fresh salmon instead of tuna——it's almost as good!

Spice-Seared Cervena Venison with Apple-Turnip Conserve, Marinated Leeks, and Caramel Jus

Serves 6

This is another terrific appetizer to prepare when entertaining. The venison can be seasoned and the vegetables cooked and dressed early in the day, the caramel *jus* made up to 1 week in advance, and the conserve made up to 2 weeks in advance. Even the plates can be assembled in advance, leaving only the venison to be seared and sliced at the last minute. Add to this the benefits of venison's low-fat, low-cholesterol profile and you have a perfect first course!

¼ pound mesclun (or other tender, young lettuces or greens)
3 medium leeks
Approximately 1 ½ cups Chicken Stock (page 189)
1 medium carrot
2 tablespoons olive oil
1 tablespoon red wine vinegar
Coarse salt
Pepper
8 cloves Roasted Garlic (page 197)
1 teaspoon cracked black pepper
½ teaspoon ground coriander
½ teaspoon ground allspice
6 well-trimmed 3-ounce, 2 × 2-inch squares venison leg meat
1 tablespoon vegetable oil
1 recipe Apple-Turnip Conserve (recipe follows)
1 recipe Caramel Jus (recipe follows)

Wash mesclun and dry it well. Wrap in damp paper towels and refrigerate until ready to use.

Trim leeks of all green parts. Split them in half, lengthwise, and wash well to remove all grit. Pat dry. Place in a small saucepan with chicken stock to cover over medium-high heat. Simmer gently for about 10 minutes, or until tender. Remove from heat and drain well. Place them in a shallow container and set aside.

Trim and peel carrot. Cut it crosswise, into ¼-inch-thick discs. Place in a small saucepan with water to cover over medium-high heat. Simmer gently for about 3 minutes, or until crisp-tender. Remove from heat and drain well. Pat dry. Add to the leeks.

A NOTE FROM JUDIE

With this recipe, the home cook gets a chance to shine. The presentation says "I really worked," but the fact that the components can be made at different stages makes it possible to be relaxed at mealtime.

The conserve can be made up to 2 weeks in advance of use. Store, covered and refrigerated. Any leftover conserve can be used to garnish other meats or poultry or to season sandwich fillings.

The caramel *jus* can be made up to 1 week in advance of use. Store, covered and refrigerated. Bring to room temperature and shake well before using. If *jus* is too thick, place it in a hot-water bath to loosen.

Whisk together olive oil, vinegar, and salt and pepper to taste. Push roasted garlic from its skin and beat it into the vinaigrette. When well combined, pour over the vegetables. Gently toss to combine. Set aside.

Combine cracked pepper, coriander, allspice, and coarse salt to taste. Generously season the venison with the spice mixture. Heat vegetable oil in a medium sauté pan over high heat. When very hot, add the seasoned venison. Sear for about 4 minutes, or until all sides are nicely browned but interior remains rare. Remove from heat and let rest for 5 minutes.

Remove greens from refrigerator. Place equal portions on each of 6 plates. Place equal portions of dressed leeks and carrot discs on top of greens. Place a small mound of apple-turnip conserve at the top of each plate. Just before serving, slice each venison cube, against the grain, into 4 or 5 slices. Fan slices out on top of the greens. Drizzle a bit of caramel *jus* across the top and serve warm.

Apple-Turnip Conserve

2 tablespoons mustard seeds
1 pound Rome apples
1 pound white turnips
3 tablespoons grapeseed oil
3 tablespoons pure maple syrup
1 tablespoon chopped fresh parsley
Coarse salt
Freshly ground pepper

Place mustard seeds in a small sauté pan over medium-high heat. Cook, shaking the pan frequently, for about 3 minutes, or until seeds have begun to emit their aroma and are lightly toasted. Remove from heat and set aside.

Peel and core apples. Peel and trim turnips. Separately cut them into ¼-inch dice. Measure out equal portions and set aside. You should have about 4 cups of each.

Heat 1½ tablespoons of the oil in a medium-sized, nonstick saucepan over medium heat. Add the diced apple, and sauté for about 5 minutes, or until slightly caramelized. Scrape from the pan and reserve.

Add remaining 1½ tablespoons of oil to the pan. Place over medium heat and stir in the turnip. Cook, stirring frequently, for about 5 minutes, or until just tender. Stir in the syrup and cook for 2 minutes. Add the reserved caramelized apple along with the parsley and salt and pepper to taste. Toss to combine. Remove from heat and scrape into a nonreactive container. Cover and place in the refrigerator for at least 2 hours, or until well chilled.

Caramel Jus

3 tablespoons sugar
½ cup Chicken Stock (page 189)
¼ cup Worcestershire sauce
4 peppercorns
¼ cup extra-virgin olive oil

Place sugar in a small, nonstick saucepan over medium heat. Cook, stirring frequently, for about 4 minutes, or until well caramelized and medium dark-brown in color. Add stock, Worcestershire, and peppercorns. Cook, stirring occasionally, for about 7 minutes, or until reduced by two-thirds. Whisk in the oil. Remove pan from heat and strain through a fine sieve or cheesecloth. Pour into a squirt bottle such as those used for catsup and mustard in luncheonettes. Store, covered, at room temperature until ready to use. Shake well before using.

SUGGESTED WINE: A hearty Pinot Noir, such as Domaine Drouhin

Wild Mushroom Minestrone
with Mascarpone Dumplings

Serves 6

This soup is so rich and delicious that you need not feel obligated to make the dumplings. If you do, however, you will have prepared a truly memorable dish. This soup is a perfect combination of earthy and sweet flavors that could easily be served as a filling main-course dish for 4 people, accompanied by a loaf of crusty Italian bread and a salad of bitter greens.

8 cups Chicken Stock (page 189)
1 Sachet (page 197)
1 ½ bulbs Roasted Garlic (page 197)
2 tablespoons olive oil
½ cup carrots in ¼-inch dice
½ cup Napa cabbage in ½-inch dice
½ cup spinach in ½-inch dice
2 tablespoons unsalted butter
¾ cup quartered fresh morels
¾ cup split fresh chanterelles
¾ cup fresh oyster mushrooms in ½-inch dice
½ cup peeled, seeded, and diced tomato
3 tablespoons chopped fresh basil
Coarse salt
Pepper
1 recipe Mascarpone Dumplings (recipe follows)
3 tablespoons freshly grated Parmesan cheese

Place the stock, sachet, and roasted garlic in a stockpot over medium-high heat. Bring to a boil. Immediately lower heat and gently simmer for 40 minutes, or until liquid is reduced by one-third. Strain through a fine sieve into a clean saucepan. Set aside.

Heat olive oil in a large sauté pan over medium heat. Add the carrot and sauté for 6 minutes. Stir in the cabbage and sauté for another 5 minutes. Add the spinach and sauté for 3 minutes. Scrape the vegetables into the reduced stock. Place pot over very low heat.

Place a large pot of salted water to boil over high heat.

Place butter in the same pan in which you sautéed the vegetables. Place over medium heat. When butter is melted, add all of the mushrooms and sauté for about 5 minutes, or until slightly softened. Stir in the tomato, basil, and salt and pepper to taste. Raise heat and shake pan to toss mixture for about 1 minute. Scrape into the stock mixture. Taste soup and adjust seasoning with salt and pepper. Raise heat to bring soup just to a simmer.

Lay out 6 warm, flat soup bowls.

When salted water is boiling, add dumplings and boil for 2 minutes, or until tender. Using a slotted spoon, lift out 3 dumplings at a time, and shake to drain off water. Place 3 dumplings in each of the soup bowls. Ladle equal portions of soup over the dumplings in each bowl. Sprinkle with Parmesan cheese and serve immediately.

NOTE: If you can't find all of the mushrooms called for in this recipe, use a combination of whatever types you can find. If only button mushrooms are available, use ¼ cup of dried porcini mushrooms that have been reconstituted in some of the reduced chicken stock. Strain and return the stock to the pot to ensure a rich mushroom flavor.

Mascarpone Dumplings

Makes 20

Since these can be made early in the day, they are an easy last-minute addition to a soup broth.

> 1 sheet fresh Semolina Pasta dough (page 191) or commercially prepared fresh
>   pasta dough
> 1 large egg
> ½ cup mascarpone cheese
> Coarse salt
> Pepper

Cut pasta dough into 1½-inch squares. Cover with a clean, damp kitchen towel to keep it from drying out.

Using a fork, beat egg in a small bowl. Set aside.

Mix mascarpone with salt and pepper to taste.

Line a small baking sheet with parchment paper.

Lay the pasta squares out in a single layer on a clean, flat surface. Using a pastry brush, lightly coat each square with the egg. Place ½ tablespoon of mascarpone in the center of each square. Fold pasta over cheese to make a triangle. Pinch edges together to seal them closed. Pull the 2 corner tips up to form a dumpling shape. Place on prepared baking sheet in a cool, dry place until ready to cook as directed in master recipe.

Butternut Squash Soup

Your guests will never guess that this soup has no cream. Smooth, slightly sweet yet spicy, this easy-to-prepare soup needs no fattening additions to have diners asking for more. At Aureole, however, we serve this soup with a large cheese-filled ravioli floating in the center—a delicious and rich addition, but it really is a lot of extra work for the home cook.

> 3 large butternut squash
> 1 large onion
> 4½ cups Chicken Stock (page 189)
> Approximately ¾ cup honey
> 2 tablespoons minced fresh savory
> ¼ teaspoon ground nutmeg
> ¼ teaspoon ground cinnamon
> ¼ teaspoon ground cardamom
> Coarse salt
> Pepper
> 2 tablespoons minced fresh chives

Peel and seed squash. Cut into ¾-inch dice. Measure out ½ cup and cut it into ¼-inch dice. Set the ¾-inch pieces aside. Place the ¼-inch pieces in a small pan of boiling water and cook for 1 minute, or until crisp-tender. Drain well and refresh under cold running water. Pat dry and set aside.

Peel onion and cut into ¾-inch dice. Combine with uncooked squash in a steamer basket over boiling water. Steam for 10 minutes, or until very tender.

While squash is steaming, heat stock in a medium saucepan over medium-high heat.

When squash and onion are tender, scrape into the bowl of a food processor fitted with the metal blade. Add half of the honey and the savory and spices and process until smooth. Slowly add stock and process until well blended. Taste and adjust seasoning with remaining honey and salt and pepper. (The amount of honey required to give this soup its dusky-sugar taste will depend on the ripeness of the squash. A very ripe squash will carry its own deep, sweet flavor, while one that is underripe will be flat and bland.) This may have to be done in batches. If necessary, after all soup has been pureed, return to saucepan over medium heat and cook for a minute or two, or until very hot.

Pour equal portions into each of 6 warm soup bowls. Garnish with reserved blanched squash and chives. Serve immediately.

A NOTE FROM JUDIE

The ravioli are wonderful, but not only do they add work, they add extra calories. If you really insist on adding them, cut twelve 3-inch circles from a fresh pasta sheet (see page 191). Mix together ½ cup farmer cheese, 1 tablespoon grated Parmesan cheese, 1 egg yolk, and salt and pepper to taste. Place a heaping tablespoonful in the center of each of 6 pasta circles. Brush the edge with an egg wash (1 large egg whisked with 2 tablespoons water) and press the remaining circles on top of each filled circle. Crimp edges to seal. Just before you are ready to serve the soup, cook the ravioli for about 2 minutes in rapidly boiling salted water. Drain well and place in the center of each warm soup bowl.

Chilled Beefsteak Tomato Soup with Goat Cheese Croutons

This soup is as refreshingly delicious as the tomatoes from which it is made. Therefore, save it for a hot midsummer's day when tomatoes are perfection and you need an icy-cold pick-me-up to start a meal.

6 large, very ripe beefsteak tomatoes
3 tablespoons extra-virgin olive oil
1 cup finely chopped yellow onion
½ cup chopped celery
1 tablespoon minced garlic
8 fresh basil leaves, washed and torn in half
2 cups sparkling mineral water
1 Sachet (page 197)
2 teaspoons Worcestershire sauce
Coarse salt
Freshly ground white pepper
1 baguette
½ pound fresh goat cheese
2 tablespoons chopped fresh basil
6 sprigs fresh basil

Peel, seed, and chop tomatoes. Heat oil in a large, heavy saucepan over medium heat. Add the onion, celery, garlic, and halved basil leaves. Lower heat and sauté for about 4 minutes, or until vegetables are just beginning to soften but do not yet have any color. Add tomato, sparkling water, and sachet. Raise heat and bring to a boil. Lower heat and simmer for 15 minutes. Remove from heat and, using a metal spoon, carefully skim off any foam. Set aside for about 30 minutes to cool slightly. Remove and discard sachet.

Place the mixture in a blender, in batches, and puree until quite smooth. Pour into a fine sieve and strain into a nonreactive bowl, pushing on solids to extract the juices. Stir in Worcestershire sauce and salt and pepper to taste. Cover with plastic film and refrigerate for at least 4 hours, or until icy-cold.

Cut the baguette, crosswise on the diagonal, into eighteen ¾-inch slices. Mash the goat cheese so that it is spreadable. Generously coat one side of each slice of bread with cheese. Sprinkle with chopped basil and salt and pepper to taste. Place on a baking sheet in oven preheated to 400°F and bake for 5 minutes, or until lightly browned on the bottom. Remove from oven and set aside.

Pour equal portions of chilled soup into each of 6 chilled, flat soup bowls. Garnish each with a sprig of fresh basil. Pass warm croutons on the side.

A NOTE FROM JUDIE

The sparkling mineral water adds a slightly different zing to a fresh-tomato soup and eliminates the need for cream to smooth out the flavor.

If the tomatoes aren't quite sweet enough to blend into the mineral water, add a touch of honey or maple syrup to counteract the acidity and balance the flavor.

Since this recipe calls for very sweet ripe tomatoes, if beefsteak aren't available, replace them with any other tomato that is very ripe. A beefsteak tomato will usually weigh about ½ pound, so you will need about 3 to 3½ pounds of other tomatoes. One pound of fresh tomatoes will usually yield about 1½ cups chopped.

New Potato and Leek Potage with Oregon Morels

Serves 6

A *potage*, in French cooking, is a soup that is pureed and enriched with cream or egg yolks. Not as thick as a classic *soupe*, it is nevertheless dense and luxurious. In this soup the pureed potatoes combine with the heady morels to make a classic *potage* consistency and flavor without the usual cream enrichment.

6 large Red Bliss potatoes (or other waxy new potatoes)
4 large leeks
½ pound fresh Oregon morels
8 cups Chicken Stock (page 189)
2 tablespoons extra-virgin olive oil
1 cup white wine
1 Sachet (page 197)
Coarse salt
Pepper
3 tablespoons chopped fresh tarragon

Peel potatoes and cut in half. Set aside.

Trim off all green parts from the leeks. Split them in half, lengthwise, and wash thoroughly. Roughly chop them and set aside.

Trim stems from morels and reserve for another use. Brush any debris from the morels and set them aside.

Place the stock in a large saucepan over high heat. Bring to a boil and add the morels. Reduce heat and simmer for 2 minutes. Remove from heat. Using a slotted spoon, lift out morels. Reserve stock and morels separately.

Heat oil in a large saucepan over medium heat. Add the potatoes and leeks and sauté for 10 minutes, or until just slightly softened. Stir in the wine, sachet, and salt and pepper to taste. Bring to a simmer and cook for 2 minutes. Stir in the reserved stock and cook for 25 minutes, or until potatoes are mushy. Remove and discard sachet.

Remove *potage* from heat. Using a handheld immersible blender, puree in the saucepan until smooth (see Note). Taste and adjust seasoning with salt and pepper. Return to medium-high heat and bring to a boil. Immediately stir in reserved morels and tarragon and remove from heat. Serve immediately in warm soup bowls.

In 1995 Charlie and his friends at California's Iron Horse Vineyards collaborated to produce a wine to be served exclusively at Aureole. A robust sparkling wine, Aureole Cuvée is a perfect accompaniment to a wide range of dishes—everything from New Potato and Leek Potage to lighter game bird dishes.

A NOTE FROM JUDIE

Charlie often stirs Duck Confit (page 191) into this *potage* for a really luxurious taste. If you just happen to have some on hand, add ½ cup when you add the morels at the end.

If you don't have a handheld immersible blender (not a mixer), push the potatoes through a fine sieve or through the fine disc of a food mill. Do not puree them in an electric blender or food processor as the heat and speed will make the potatoes starchy.

Cold Lobster and Sauternes Cream

Serves 6

This soup always elicits "oohs" and "aahs" and "Just what are these unusual flavors?" It is truly an extravaganza of flavors—succulent lobster, elegant Sauternes, and butterfat-rich cream—that is not for the faint-hearted!

5 shallots
2 medium carrots
2 medium onions
3 bulbs fennel
3 tablespoons olive oil
1 tablespoon minced fresh tarragon
1 Sachet (page 197)
4 cups Sauternes
4 cups heavy cream
4 cups hot Shellfish Stock made with lobster (page 190)
Coarse salt
Pepper
1¼ cups diced cooked lobster meat
6 sprigs fresh tarragon

A NOTE FROM JUDIE

Make the lobster stock after you've had a midsummer lobster feast. Or, cook up lobsters and use the shells and some of the meat for this recipe and use the remaining meat for lobster cocktails (see page 18) or lobster salad. This soup will keep for no more than 3 days in the refrigerator or 3 weeks in the freezer, so plan a dinner party around it.

Peel shallots, carrots, and onions. Trim fennel. Cut all the vegetables into a very fine dice.

Heat oil in a large saucepan over medium heat. Add diced vegetables, tarragon, and sachet. Lower heat and allow the vegetables to sweat their moisture for about 15 minutes, or until translucent. Stir in the wine and bring to a simmer. Cook for about 15 minutes, or until reduced by half. Remove from heat and reserve.

While wine is reducing, place cream in a medium saucepan over medium heat. Bring to a simmer and cook for about 20 minutes, or until reduced by half. Watch carefully so that the cream does not boil, as it will easily overflow, as well as scorch and/or break.

Combine the reserved wine reduction with the hot stock in a large saucepan over medium heat. Bring to a boil. Lower heat and simmer for 15 minutes, or until reduced by one-third. Strain through a fine sieve into a clean saucepan. Using a handheld immersible blender (not a mixer), blend the reduced cream into the stock mixture. Taste and adjust seasoning with salt and pepper. Remove from heat and place in an ice-water bath to cool quickly. Scrape into a nonporous container, cover, and refrigerate until well chilled.

When ready to serve, mix in diced lobster. Pour equal portions into each of 6 well-chilled, flat-rimmed soup bowls. Garnish with a fresh tarragon sprig and serve icy-cold.

II. FROM THE GARDEN: SALADS AND SIDE DISHES

Nowhere in cooking does seasonality play a more important role than during the preparation of salads and side dishes. In these dishes you want to capture the ingredients at the peak moment of taste and composition so that the layers of freshness combine with complex accents to create a perfectly balanced plate.

In the restaurants, we have a wealth of purveyors meeting our demand for the best. A home cook has the opportunity to control ingredients through backyard gardens, farmers' markets, specialty stores, and mail-order sources. Just remember, the result will only be as good as the basic ingredients.

A continuing debate rages about whether organically grown produce is better than that grown with chemical fertilizers and other enhancements. For the health of our children and the planet, organically grown is by far the best. But organically grown does not always mean fresh and flavorful. Fresh, locally grown produce often has much more flavor than shipped-in organically grown. Almost all commercially grown products, whether organic or not, have had their seasons altered to meet year-round demand. This constant accessibility has depleted the naturally deep flavors, as well as the textural compositions, of many of our more familiar fruits, berries, and vegetables. To ensure quality, buy the best of whatever is in season at the moment. Use your taste buds to determine substitutions when the produce called for is not available. The recipe won't be the same, but it will probably be just as good and perhaps even better.

When you can, buy from local farmers. Develop a farmers' market with the help of your state department of agriculture. Grow your own. Even a city window box, fire escape, or terrace can yield fresh herbs and tomatoes. Start with the freshest, most flavorful produce available and you will be surprised at how little work is required to create a memorable salad or side dish.

SALADS

Wilted Arugula and Roasted Walnut Salad with Warm Goat Cheese Fondue

Warm Porcini and Mesclun Salad with Tomato Vinaigrette

Preserved Duck Salad Roulade with Roquefort Vinaigrette

Crisped Sweetbread Salad

Composed Salad of Sautéed Shrimp and Couscous

Sautéed Skate Wing and Lentil Salad with Melted Leeks

Dungeness Crab and New Potato Salad

Yellowfin Tuna Carpaccio with Spicy Greens

SIDE DISHES

Crisp Potato-Eggplant Tart

Potato Galette

Basil-Essenced Potatoes

Leeks and New Potatoes

Garlic Spinach

Ratatouille

Butternut Squash Flan

Wilted Arugula and Roasted Walnut Salad with Warm Goat Cheese Fondue

Serves 6

This simple salad can be served all year round—simply substitute spicy fall and winter greens for the arugula.

1 Granny Smith apple
½ teaspoon fresh lemon juice
3 bunches arugula (see Note)
4 ½ ounces fresh goat cheese
3 tablespoons heavy cream
⅜ cup walnut oil
3 tablespoons white wine vinegar
Coarse salt
Pepper
24 toasted walnut halves

Peel and core apple. Cut into fine julienne. Toss with lemon juice to keep it from discoloring. Cover until ready to use.

Wash and dry arugula. Pick off any discolored parts. Set aside.

Combine goat cheese and cream in a small saucepan over low heat. Cook, stirring constantly, until smooth and well combined. Remove from heat.

Toss arugula with oil and vinegar and salt and pepper to taste. Arrange equal portions of the dressed arugula on each of 6 chilled salad plates. Randomly place 4 walnut halves and equal portions of the reserved apple julienne over the arugula. Drizzle the warm goat cheese mixture over the salad in a crisscross pattern (see photograph on page 46). Serve immediately.

Warm Porcini and Mesclun Salad with Tomato Vinaigrette

Serves 6

Porcini, known as *cèpes* in France, are meaty, earthy-tasting wild mushrooms now cultivated in the United States. The firm, pale brown to cream *boletus edulis* has a pungent flavor that makes it one of the world's most revered mushrooms.

4 very ripe medium tomatoes
½ cup olive oil
1 tablespoon balsamic vinegar
Coarse salt
Pepper
12 chives
½ pound mesclun
1 ½ pounds fresh porcini mushrooms
1 cup Tomato Vinaigrette (page 195)

Peel, core, and quarter tomatoes. Remove the seeds and membranes and trim ends so that the tomato pieces will lie flat. Place them in a nonreactive bowl and toss with 2 tablespoons of olive oil, the balsamic vinegar, and salt and pepper to taste.

Wash and dry chives. Cut them into 1-inch pieces and set aside.

Wash and dry mesclun. Place in a mixing bowl and set aside.

Using a pastry brush, gently clean mushrooms of any dirt particles. Trim off any blemishes and slice, randomly, into ¼-inch-thick pieces.

Heat 3 tablespoons of olive oil in a heavy, nonstick sauté pan over medium heat. Add half of the porcini. Season to taste with salt and pepper and sauté for about 2 minutes, or until golden. Scrape from pan onto a paper towel to drain. Place the remaining 3 tablespoons of oil in the same pan and proceed as above to sauté and drain remaining porcini.

Toss mesclun with half of the tomato vinaigrette. Mound equal portions in the center of each of 6 luncheon plates. Place equal portions of the mushrooms evenly over the top of the greens. Place 2 marinated tomato circles opposite each other on two sides of the plate. Drizzle remaining vinaigrette over all. Sprinkle with chives and serve while porcini are warm.

SUGGESTED WINE: A Rhone wine, such as Côte Rôtie Delas

A NOTE FROM JUDIE

When purchasing porcini, select those that are very firm, with a pale spongy layer beneath the cap. Oregon-grown porcini are now readily available throughout the United States, but some feel that they lack the intense flavor of those imported from Europe. Whichever you use, remember that they absorb oil rapidly and can dry and burn quickly. Therefore, either cook them very slowly over very low heat, quickly sauté them, or incorporate them into sauces. Store fresh, firm porcini, refrigerated, in a single layer on a tray lined with paper towel. If you change the towel daily, the porcini should keep for about 1 week.

Preserved Duck Salad Roulade with Roquefort Vinaigrette

Serves 6

The unusual lettuce jackets for these salad rolls provide an interesting presentation despite their rather ordinary origins. Duck confit is a great pantry item, as it adds an exotic flavor to simple dishes.

12 romaine lettuce leaves
1 small head frisee
2 teaspoons vegetable oil
2 tablespoons minced shallots
1 recipe Duck Confit (page 191)
¾ cup julienned fresh tomato
1 cup Red Wine–Shallot Vinaigrette (page 193)
¾ cup crumbled Roquefort cheese
1 tablespoon chopped fresh parsley
Coarse salt
Pepper

Bring a medium saucepan of water to boil over high heat. Add the romaine leaves and cook for 5 seconds, or until just blanched. Drain and refresh in an ice-water bath. Pat dry. Trim off any hard ribs and rough edges. Lay out in a single layer on a sheet of waxed paper. Cover with paper towel and pat down to absorb any remaining moisture.

Pull frisee apart. Wash and dry. Place in a bowl and set aside.

Heat oil in a small sauté pan over medium heat. Add shallots. Lower heat and cook for about 4 minutes, or just until the shallots have sweated most of their moisture. Scrape into the frisee. Toss to combine. Add the confit, tomato, and 2 tablespoons of the vinaigrette and toss to blend.

Uncover the romaine leaves. Use 2 leaves to make each roulade: Place them together on a flat work surface, with an edge slightly overlapping to make a rather rectangular piece. If necessary, trim to make even. Place equal portions of duck salad across the center of the leaves, leaving a 1½- to 2-inch leaf edge all around. Fold in the ends and then the sides to form a solid cylindrical shape. Cut each cylinder in half, crosswise, on the diagonal. Place 1 cylinder on each of 6 chilled plates, placing the uncut sides back to back with the diagonal cuts pointing in opposite directions.

Heat the remaining vinaigrette over very low heat. Whisk in the cheese and parsley. Taste and adjust seasoning with salt and pepper. Spoon equal portions over the salad cylinders. Serve immediately.

SUGGESTED WINE: A Beaujolais

A NOTE FROM JUDIE

The most important steps in making this salad are the quick blanching of the leaves——you want them neither too soft nor too firm——and the trimming and overlapping to make a neat shape to enfold the filling. The salad cylinders can be made early in the day and stored, covered and refrigerated, until ready to serve.

Be sure to use true Roquefort cheese for this vinaigrette. Its creamy texture and pungent, rather salty flavor make a perfect foil to the rich confit.

You could use spinach leaves in place of the romaine and shredded grilled chicken breast in place of the confit.

Crisped Sweetbread Salad

Serves 6

All of the components of this salad can be readied for cooking and assembling long before it is put together, so it makes an especially inviting dinner-party first course. It is so well balanced, however, that it could also serve as a luncheon main course.

1 ½ pounds fresh veal sweetbreads
3 tablespoons coarse salt plus more to taste
3 tablespoons white vinegar
3 heads baby oak leaf lettuce
½ pound fresh haricots verts or baby string beans
6 large button mushrooms
2 shallots
2 large eggs
1 cup plus 2 tablespoons all-purpose flour
Pinch ground nutmeg
Freshly ground pepper
6 tablespoons corn oil
1 cup Truffle Vinaigrette (page 194)
6 oval Potato Gaufrettes (page 192)

A NOTE FROM JUDIE

If you don't want to splurge on truffle vinaigrette, replace it with any of the other vinaigrettes (see pages 193-195). You could also replace the sweetbreads with turkey, chicken, or veal medallions. The salad base could also be served as a side salad.

Place sweetbreads in a deep bowl with ice water to cover. Refrigerate for at least 8 hours. Drain well, then rinse under cold running water. Place in a medium saucepan with cold water to cover over medium-high heat. Add 3 tablespoons of coarse salt and the vinegar and bring to a boil. Lower heat and gently simmer for 12 minutes. Immediately remove from heat and drain well. Place in an ice-water bath and soak for 4 minutes, or until cold in the center. Drain well and trim off any fat or sinew.

Line a small baking sheet with a clean kitchen towel. Place cleaned sweetbreads on the towel. Place another tray of equal size on top of the sweetbreads. Place a weight of at least 3 pounds on top. Refrigerate the weighted sweetbreads for at least 8 hours.

Pull the lettuce apart. Wash and dry well. Wrap in damp paper towel and refrigerate until ready to use.

If necessary, trim the beans. Wash them well. Place them in boiling water to cover and cook for 4 minutes, or until crisp-tender but still bright green. Immediately drain and refresh in an ice-water bath. Pat dry and set aside.

Remove stems from mushrooms. Brush off any debris and cut, vertically, into paper-thin slices. Set aside.

Peel and mince shallots. Set them aside.

Place the eggs in a flat bowl and, using a fork, lightly beat.

Combine 1 cup of flour, the nutmeg, and salt and pepper to taste in another flat bowl.

Lightly coat a plate with the remaining 2 tablespoons of flour.

Remove pressed sweetbreads from the refrigerator. Remove the weight and top tray. Using a very sharp knife, cut sweetbreads, vertically, into ½- to ¾-inch-thick medallions. Dredge each medallion in the seasoned flour. Dip into the egg and then coat in a final layer of seasoned flour. Place coated medallions on the floured plate as they are finished.

Line a baking sheet with paper towels and set it beside the stove.

Heat oil in a large, nonstick sauté pan over medium-high heat. Add the prepared sweetbreads and cook for 3 minutes, or until golden. Turn and cook for 2 minutes, or until golden. If necessary, cook in two batches so that pan is not crowded. Place cooked sweetbreads on the paper-lined tray to drain for a minute.

Place the lettuce, *haricots verts*, mushrooms, and shallots in a large bowl. Drizzle with 2 tablespoons of vinaigrette and toss to combine. Mound equal portions of salad in the center of each of 6 well-chilled plates. Slightly overlap 2 sweetbread medallions on top of each of the salads. Spoon vinaigrette over all. Lean a *gaufrette* on the side and serve immediately.

SUGGESTED WINE: A white Burgundy, such as St. Aubin or Rully

Composed Salad of Sautéed Shrimp and Couscous

Serves 6

A taste of curry from India, nutritious couscous from North Africa, and everybody's favorite, shrimp, make this a truly American, melting-pot salad.

18 large shrimp, peeled and deveined
6 tablespoons olive oil
2 tablespoons fresh lime juice
2 tablespoons chopped fresh tarragon
½ tablespoon freshly ground black pepper plus more to taste
1 ½ cups quick-cooking couscous
½ cup diced red onion
½ cup peeled, seeded, and diced tomato
2 ¼ cups Chicken Stock (page 189)
1 cup Curry Vinaigrette (page 194)
½ cup Brunoise (see page 197)
Coarse salt
1 recipe Crispy Leeks (page 193)
12 to 18 small red lettuce leaves (or other colorful lettuce), washed and dried

Combine shrimp with 4 tablespoons of olive oil, lime juice, tarragon, and ½ tablespoon pepper in a nonreactive bowl. Cover and refrigerate for at least 2 hours.

Place couscous in a heatproof bowl. Set aside.

Heat remaining 2 tablespoons of olive oil in a medium saucepan over medium heat. Add the red onion and sauté for 2 minutes. Stir in the tomato and then the stock. Bring to a boil. Immediately remove from heat and pour over the couscous. Stir to combine. Cover with plastic film and set aside to steam.

Combine vinaigrette and *brunoise*. Taste and adjust seasoning with salt and pepper. Set aside.

Lay leeks on a baking sheet and place in a 175°F oven to warm.

Line a baking sheet with paper towels. Remove shrimp from the refrigerator. Season to taste with salt. Heat a medium sauté pan over medium-high heat. Add half of the shrimp and cook for 1½ to 2 minutes per side, or until just cooked. Place the shrimp on prepared sheet and proceed to cook and drain remaining shrimp as above.

Using a fork, fluff the couscous. Taste and adjust seasoning with salt and pepper. Mound equal portions in the center of each of 6 warm plates. Place 3 shrimp on top. Arrange lettuce leaves around the edge of the plate. Spoon vinaigrette over all. Finish with a mound of leeks on top of the shrimp. Serve immediately.

SUGGESTED WINE: An exotic white wine, such as Caymus Conundrum

A NOTE FROM JUDIE

A home cook's dream! The shrimp can be marinating, the couscous steaming, and the leeks fried long before your guests arrive. This salad is so easy to put together and so nutritious, it could nicely fit into the weekly menu.

Couscous, the granular wheat staple of North Africa, absorbs flavors with enthusiasm, so it makes a wonderful bed for other aromatic foods. You could, if you don't have it on hand, use any other grain for the base of this salad. When finishing this plate, it is especially important to look for a balance of color and texture.

Sautéed Skate Wing and Lentil Salad with Melted Leeks

This is another salad that would make a wonderful main course. The recipe could easily be doubled for a filling meal for 6. If you can't find green lentils and skate, use regular lentils and any other firm-fleshed white fish. Whatever you use, it is important that neither the lentils nor the fish be overcooked.

1 medium carrot

1 stalk celery

1 cup dried green lentils

3 ¼ cups Chicken Stock (page 189)

1 clove garlic, peeled

1 Sachet (page 197)

5 tablespoons olive oil

1 tablespoon red wine vinegar

2 tablespoons roughly chopped fresh parsley

Coarse salt

Pepper

3 large leeks

2 medium skate wings or six 3- to 4-ounce cleaned skate pieces

⅔ cup superfine flour (such as Wondra)

¼ cup safflower or corn oil

12 spears endive, washed and dried

1 ¼ cups Balsamic Vinaigrette (page 195)

6 sprigs fresh Italian parsley

Peel carrot. Cut it, crosswise, into ¼-inch-thick rounds. Measure out ½ cup and set aside. Reserve remaining carrot for another use.

Wash celery. Peel off stringy skin and cut it, crosswise, into ¼-inch-thick slices. Measure out ½ cup and set aside. Reserve remaining celery for another use.

Rinse lentils and remove any debris. Combine with 3 cups of chicken stock, the garlic, and the sachet in a medium saucepan over medium-high heat. Bring to a simmer. Lower heat and simmer for 20 minutes, or until lentils just begin to soften. Add the carrot and celery slices. Simmer for an additional 12 minutes, shaking pan from time to time to prevent sticking, or until all of the moisture is absorbed and lentils are tender. Add water, a bit at a time, if necessary. Remove from heat and discard sachet. Stir in 3 tablespoons of olive oil, the vinegar, parsley, and salt and pepper to taste. Allow to marinate and come to room temperature.

Trim leeks of all green parts. Split them in half, lengthwise, and rinse thoroughly under cold running water. Pat dry. Heat the remaining 2 tablespoons of olive oil in a medium sauté pan over medium-low heat. Add leeks, remaining ¼ cup of chicken stock, and salt and pepper to taste. Cook, stirring frequently, for about 25 minutes, or until leeks are very limp and almost melted. Remove from heat and allow to come to room temperature.

If you have not had your fishmonger clean the skate wings into pieces, proceed as follows: Using a very sharp boning knife, follow the flesh from the rib side out (*top right*), carefully lifting the flesh on each side. Remove skin and trim the edges of all sinew. Slice into 3- to 4-ounce portions by cutting vertically with the grain (*center right*). Score the edges to keep flesh from curling as it cooks (*bottom right*). Place fish on a thick layer of paper towels. Cover with another layer of paper towels and press to release as much moisture as possible. Remove towels.

Season the skate with salt and pepper to taste. Liberally dust seasoned fish with flour. Heat the safflower oil in a large, nonstick sauté pan over medium-high heat. Add the seasoned skate and cook for 4 minutes per side, or until nicely browned. Remove from pan and drain on paper towels.

Place 2 endive spears at the center of each of 6 plates, pointed ends facing outward. Mound equal portions of the lentil salad in the center of each plate, partially covering endive base. Randomly place melted leeks around the edge of the plate. Lay a piece of skate on top of the lentils and spoon vinaigrette over the top and around the leeks. Garnish with a parsley sprig and serve immediately.

SUGGESTED WINE: Pouilly Fumé or Fumé Blanc

Dungeness Crab and
New Potato Salad

Serves 6

Summer's sweet crab turns this into a very special "not picnic style" potato salad. It would make a superb main course for a special-occasion lunch or brunch.

1 pound fresh Dungeness crab
1 ½ pounds Red Bliss potatoes
Coarse salt
2 leeks
1 ½ tablespoons olive oil
1 tablespoon minced fresh parsley
Freshly ground pepper
1 ½ cups mizuna
2 ounces Osetra caviar
¾ cup Citrus Vinaigrette (page 193)
6 Herb-Potato Maximes (page 192)

Pick through the crab to remove any shell or cartilage. Place in a bowl. Cover and refrigerate until ready to use.

Peel potatoes. Place in a medium saucepan with water to cover. Add salt to taste and place over high heat. Bring to a boil. Lower heat and simmer for 20 minutes, or until tender. Drain well. Set aside and allow to rest until cool enough to handle. When cool, cut, crosswise, into ¼-inch-thick slices. Set aside.

Trim leeks of all green parts. Cut them in half, lengthwise, and wash well under cold running water. Pat dry. Slice, crosswise, into very fine pieces. Heat the olive oil in a medium sauté pan over medium heat. Add leeks and cook for about 5 minutes, or until they have sweated their moisture and are transparent. Stir in the potatoes and parsley. Remove from heat and season to taste with salt and pepper. Scrape into a bowl. Cover and refrigerate for about 2 hours, or until well chilled.

Wash and dry the mizuna. Set aside.

When ready to serve, place a 3½-inch ring mold in the center of each of 6 chilled plates. Place equal portions of the salad in each of the molds, pushing down to make the center a bit concave. Remove the crab from the refrigerator and mound an equal portion on top of each potato ring. Carefully remove the molds. Top with equal portions of caviar. Arrange a small bunch of greens, leaves facing out from the center, on each plate. Drizzle vinaigrette over the top and around the edge. Lean a potato *maxime* against the side and serve immediately.

SUGGESTED WINE: An elegant white burgundy, such as Puligny-Montrachet Leflaive

A NOTE FROM JUDIE

If you can't find Red Bliss potatoes, use any other waxy new potato. If no mizuna is available, use mâche or any other soft, small green or tender lettuce. If you have no caviar, garnish with minced fresh herbs. Charlie says, "Keep the basics but make it your own!"

One of the elements that makes this salad special is Charlie's delicious citrus vinaigrette. Keep it on hand, stored tightly covered in the refrigerator, to add life to any number of salads, grilled fish, or poultry.

Yellowfin Tuna Carpaccio
with Spicy Greens

Serves 6

Traditionally, *carpaccio* is an Italian appetizer composed of paper-thin pieces of raw filet of beef, often drizzled with olive oil and lemon juice and garnished with onions and capers. Only premium-quality, sushi-grade yellowfin or bluefin tuna has the rich-tasting flesh needed for this *carpaccio*. The meat of yellowfin tuna is usually pale pink, while the adult bluefin has a deep red, very flavorful flesh. Either type makes great eating—raw or just barely cooked. If you've never eaten raw tuna, try this unique *carpaccio*. It is the perfect introduction to the succulent taste of this delicate, sweetly flavored fish.

> 5 cups spicy greens, such as watercress, purslane, or arugula
> Six ¼-inch-thick crosscut 3-ounce slices yellowfin tuna
> 2 tablespoons extra-virgin olive oil
> Freshly ground pepper
> ¾ cup Citrus Vinaigrette (page 193)

Wash greens and dry them thoroughly. Place in a mixing bowl and set aside.

Rub each side of the tuna medallions with a bit of the olive oil (*top right*). Season with pepper. Place a 12 × 12-inch piece of plastic film on a flat surface. Set a medallion on top and carefully lay another sheet of plastic film over it. With a meat pounder, gently flatten medallion (*center right*), turning it slightly with each stroke to get a round, uniform piece approximately ¹⁄₁₆ inch thick. Repeat process for each medallion. Refrigerate finished medallions as you work.

Drizzle about ¼ cup of the vinaigrette over the greens. Toss to coat. Place equal portions in the center of each of 6 well-chilled dinner plates. Remove the tuna from the refrigerator. One at a time, remove the top layer of plastic film (*bottom right*) and invert the medallion over the top of the greens. Carefully remove and discard the remaining piece of plastic film. Spoon remaining vinaigrette over the tuna and around the edge of each plate. Serve immediately.

SUGGESTED WINE: A Sauvignon Blanc, such as Duckhorn

Crisp Potato-Eggplant Tart

Makes one 9-inch tart

This tart is so deliciously rich, it can stand alone as a luncheon main course. A crisp green salad and a glass of nicely chilled white wine would complete a most satisfactory meal.

2 ¼ cups finely diced, peeled eggplant
1 teaspoon coarse salt plus more to taste
¼ cup plus 2 tablespoons safflower oil
3 tablespoons minced shallots
4 large Idaho potatoes
Pepper
¼ cup (½ stick) unsalted butter

Place eggplant in a nonreactive bowl. Toss with 1 teaspoon of salt and allow to sit for 20 minutes. Remove to a clean kitchen towel and tightly twist to squeeze out all moisture. Set aside.

Heat 2 tablespoons of oil in a medium sauté pan over medium heat. Add the eggplant and shallots and sauté for about 6 minutes, or until very tender. Remove from heat and set aside.

Peel potatoes. Using a hand grater or mandoline, shred potatoes into a clean kitchen towel. Tightly twist to squeeze out as much moisture as possible.

Preheat oven to 375°F.

Heat remaining ¼ cup of oil in a 9-inch ovenproof, nonstick sauté pan over medium heat. Using a spatula, evenly press half of the potatoes into the pan. Season to taste with salt and pepper. Spread the reserved eggplant over the top. Pat remaining potatoes evenly over the eggplant. Again, season to taste with salt and pepper. Cook for about 10 minutes, or until bottom is golden. Carefully turn and dab the crust with bits of butter. Cook for about 5 minutes, or until bottom begins to crisp. Place in the preheated oven and bake for 25 minutes, or until potatoes are cooked and tart is golden and crisp. Remove from oven and allow to rest for 5 minutes. Using a sharp serrated knife, cut into 6 wedges and serve immediately.

A NOTE FROM JUDIE

The salting helps leach any bitterness from the eggplant. It is imperative that you remove as much of the moisture as possible from both vegetables. For the eggplant, this ensures a sweet, dense flavor and for the potatoes, a crisp, dry crust. If you occasionally shake the pan as the bottom potato layer browns, it will keep it from sticking and will make turning the tart much easier.

Potato Galette

Serves 6

A potato *galette* is a traditional French peasant dish that can be made from either sliced raw or pureed cooked potatoes. These flat, round cakes can be made, as I have done here, in individual portions or as one large, crisp cake to be cut into wedges. Don't be concerned about the shape of the potato slices. The taste depends on the crispness of the *galette*, not how perfectly the potatoes are cut. Rustic or uniform—it's your choice.

> 5 large Idaho potatoes
> ¼ cup plus 2 tablespoons vegetable oil
> Coarse salt
> Freshly ground pepper

Peel potatoes. Wash and pat them dry. Cut potatoes, crosswise, into paper-thin slices with a mandoline or vegetable slicer.

Preheat oven to 300°F.

Heat half of the oil in a 12-inch nonstick sauté pan over medium heat. Carefully form 3 separate 4-inch-diameter circles of slightly overlapping potato slices in the hot oil. Place a slice in the center, if necessary, to make a solid disc. While bottom layer is browning, continue to layer potatoes in an overlapping circular pattern until the cakes are about ½ inch thick. Fry for 8 to 10 minutes, or until bottoms are golden brown. Season tops with salt and pepper to taste and carefully turn. Fry for another 6 to 8 minutes, or until potatoes are completely cooked and bottoms are golden. Remove to a baking sheet and place in preheated oven to keep warm. Continue to make *galettes*, as above, using remaining oil and potatoes.

Serve hot as a side dish or as a base for fish, meats, or poultry.

Basil-Essenced Potatoes

Serves 6

These potatoes work particularly well as a plate garnish when piped through a pastry bag fitted with a #8 round tip.

8 *fresh basil leaves*
2 *tablespoons olive oil*
2 *pounds waxy new potatoes*
2 *cloves garlic, peeled*
Coarse salt
Pepper

Place basil in a mortar with the olive oil. Using a pestle, pound into a puree. Scrape from mortar and set aside.

Peel and dice potatoes. Place in salted water to cover in a medium saucepan over medium heat. Add garlic and bring to a boil. Lower heat and simmer for 25 minutes, or until tender. Drain well. Pass through a ricer or food mill and beat in basil puree. Season to taste and serve warm.

A NOTE FROM JUDIE

Charlie prefers using a waxy new potato in this dish so that the mixture is a rich, creamy puree. Do not use the more familiar and fluffier russet or baking potato. If you have not used a ricer or food mill to make "mashed" potatoes, you'll be surprised at how quickly they create lump-free potatoes. These potatoes hold extremely well in the top half of a double boiler over hot water.

Leeks and New Potatoes

Serves 6

Intensely flavorful and meltingly tender, this side dish is a perfect foil for almost any meat or poultry. However, I'm partial to pairing it with duck or other game birds.

4 large leeks
12 Red Bliss potatoes
2 ½ cups Chicken Stock (page 189)
2 tablespoons olive oil
1 Sachet (page 197)
Coarse salt
Pepper

Trim leeks of all green parts. Split them in half, lengthwise. Place in cold water and swish them around to loosen grit. Drain and rinse under cold running water. Pat dry and set aside.

Wash potatoes. Cut, crosswise, into thin slices. Place in a medium saucepan along with the leeks, stock, olive oil, sachet, and salt and pepper to taste. Place over medium heat and bring to a simmer. Cover and simmer for 10 minutes. Uncover and simmer for an additional 15 minutes, or until stock has been absorbed and the vegetables are very tender. Serve hot.

Garlic Spinach

Serves 6

This spinach makes a tasty bed for many main-course fish or poultry dishes, hot or at room temperature. It could also be the base for a seafood salad.

1 ½ pounds fresh spinach
¼ cup (½ stick) unsalted butter
2 tablespoons minced shallots
1 tablespoon Roasted Garlic puree (see page 197)
Coarse salt
Pepper

Thoroughly wash, stem, and dry spinach. Melt butter in a large sauté pan over medium heat. Add shallots and garlic puree and sauté for 2 minutes, or until butter begins to brown slightly. Add spinach and salt and pepper to taste. Lower heat and sauté for 3 to 5 minutes, or until spinach is just wilted and is well coated with seasonings. Serve immediately.

A NOTE FROM JUDIE

Just lightly brown the butter——if it gets too dark, it will be sharp and burned-tasting.

Ratatouille

Serves 6 to 8

Ratatouille can, of course, be made all year long, but it will never be better than when it is made at the height of summer, when all the produce is sweet-tasting and garden-fresh. A traditional summertime dish of Provence, it can be served as a side dish or an appetizer or snack with crisp toasts or crackers. Its versatility goes even further—it tastes good hot, at room temperature, or cold. Ratatouille is a great dish to have on hand. It will keep for a week, covered and refrigerated, getting better-tasting every day. If you plan to serve it hot, be sure to make it in advance so the flavors can blend. Reheat before serving.

2 small firm eggplants (see A Note from Both of Us)
Coarse salt
2 small green zucchini
1 small yellow summer squash
1 red bell pepper
1 yellow bell pepper
1 large white Bermuda onion
8 fresh basil leaves
2 cloves garlic
¼ teaspoon sea salt
½ cup olive oil
½ cup dry white wine
⅔ cup canned tomato puree
Freshly ground pepper

Wash eggplants well. Trim off stems and cut into ½-inch dice. Place in a nonreactive bowl and liberally sprinkle with coarse salt. Set aside for at least 30 minutes.

Wash zucchini, summer squash, and peppers. Trim squash and cut them into ¼-inch dice. Core, seed, and remove membranes from peppers. Cut them into ¼-inch dice. Combine vegetables in a large mixing bowl.

Peel onion and cut into ¼-inch dice. Add to squash and peppers.

Wash and chop basil. Set aside.

Peel and chop garlic. Place in a mortar. Add sea salt and, using a pestle, mash together until almost pastelike. Set aside.

Heat the oil in a large, nonstick sauté pan over medium heat. Add the mixed diced vegetables, a bit at a time, and sauté for about 4 minutes, or just until the onion has a bit of color. Do not crowd the pan. When vegetables are sautéed, scrape them into a large, heavy-bottomed saucepan. Place eggplant in a clean towel and twist to ring out all moisture. Place eggplant in the sauté pan, adding a bit more oil if necessary, and sauté for about 4 minutes, or until slightly colored. Scrape into saucepan along with the other vegetables.

Add mashed garlic to the sauté pan and cook, stirring constantly, for about 1 minute, or until just browning. Add wine and stir to deglaze pan. Cook for 5 minutes. Stir in tomato puree and basil and cook for 2 minutes. Scrape into the vegetables.

Place saucepan over medium-high heat and bring to a simmer. Season to taste with salt and pepper and simmer slowly, adjusting the heat as necessary, for 20 minutes, or until vegetables are soft but not mushy and flavors have blended. Scrape into a medium strainer over a mixing bowl. Reserve liquid from the ratatouille. Place ratatouille in a nonporous container. Cover and refrigerate for at least 8 hours, or until well chilled.

Butternut Squash Flan

Serves 6

You could use any hard winter squash or pumpkin to make this delicate side dish. Make sure that much of the moisture is out of the squash or the flans will not set properly. If using pumpkin, canned will often work better than fresh, giving more flavor and density.

> One 1½-pound butternut squash
> Coarse salt
> 3 large eggs
> 3 large egg yolks
> ½ cup heavy cream
> White pepper
> 2 tablespoons unsalted butter, softened

Preheat oven to 250°F.

Peel and seed squash and cut it into ¾-inch dice. You will need about 1¾ cups diced squash. Place in a medium saucepan with water to cover over medium heat. Add salt to taste and bring to a boil. Lower heat and simmer for 15 minutes, or until very tender and almost falling apart. Drain well. Place on a nonstick baking sheet in preheated oven for 15 minutes, or until quite dry. Remove from heat. Raise oven temperature to 325°F.

Process eggs, egg yolks, and cream in a food processor fitted with the metal blade until well blended. Add squash and salt to taste and process until very smooth. Taste and adjust seasoning with salt and pepper.

Generously butter six 6-ounce timbales or small soufflé dishes. Pour equal portions of squash mixture into buttered molds. Place filled timbales in a baking pan large enough to hold them comfortably. Add hot water to come up halfway. Place in preheated oven and bake for 25 minutes, or until a knife inserted in the center comes out clean. Remove from oven and water bath. Allow to set, on a wire rack, for 2 to 3 minutes before unmolding onto a warm platter or plates.

III. SOME SIMPLE FOODS: PASTAS AND GRAINS

Although I am not known for my pastas and grain-based dishes, the demands of creating low-impact diets combined with the not-so-subtle intrusions of Italian and healthful cooking techniques into American dining habits have led me to some interesting experiments.

Pastas and grains are areas of modern American cuisine that have been widely influenced by the tide of immigration. Pasta incorporates not only the dried semolina and egg noodles of Italy, but also the buckwheat, rice, and bean thread noodles of Asia, the hearty spätzle and egg noodles of Europe, and the dumplings and stuffed doughs from a wide spectrum of cultures. Risotto, although traditionally made with fat, short-grained Italian rices such as Arborio, is now being made with many types of rices and grains, incorporating flavors from all over the world.

In my kitchens, I have expanded the conventional uses for these low-fat, low-cholesterol, highly nutritious traditional dishes. Soba noodle cakes are used as a base for tuna, risotto is made from multiple grains, a wide variety of stuffings are turned into ravioli, either large or small, which are often used as a garnish rather than the central component of a dish, and spätzle and gnocchi are often flavored to balance the meat, poultry, or game that they accompany.

For the home cook, the implements of pasta making are inexpensive additions to the kitchen. Hand-cranked pasta machines can be purchased for less than twenty-five dollars and are guaranteed to make wonderful pasta. These machines help you take the simple basics of soft-wheat flour and eggs and turn them into a wondrous number of shapes. I recommend them highly.

For rices and other grains, investigate ethnic markets and health-food stores to broaden your repertoire.

Ask questions about recommended methods of preparation and flavoring. This is the way a professional chef introduces new ingredients into a menu. I know that the palette of pastas and risottos we have discovered has broadened the taste, nutrition, and textures of great American cooking.

Soft Potato Ravioli with Truffle Pan Sauce

Open Ravioli of Seared Salmon and Ratatouille

Spinach Tagliatelle with Seared Scallops and Fresh Sage

Four-Herb Fettuccine with Green Vegetables and Shaved Asiago

Crisped Soba Noodle Cake

Sweet Onion-Risotto Cakes

Four-Grain Vegetable Risotto

Pumpkin Risotto with Duck Confit and Parmesan

Israeli Couscous

Vegetable Couscous

Soft Polenta

Soft Potato Ravioli with Truffle Pan Sauce

Serves 6

If I say so myself, this is a truly elegant, though slightly unorthodox, first-course pasta. It always gets raves in the dining room. Perhaps it is the combination of the lowly potato—my true love—with the exotic truffle that lifts these ravioli from the ordinary to the extraordinary.

4 cups rich Chicken Stock (see Note, page 189)
1 cup Mirepoix (page 197)
3 cloves garlic, peeled
2 pounds russet potatoes
2 tablespoons chopped onion
3 ounces fresh soft goat cheese
2 tablespoons minced fresh parsley
⅓ cup coarse salt plus more to taste
Freshly ground white pepper
2 tablespoons all-purpose flour
2 large eggs
Four 12 × 8-inch sheets fresh Semolina Pasta (page 191)
1 medium black truffle
⅓ cup truffle butter (see Note at end of recipe)
2 tablespoons minced fresh chive

Combine stock, *mirepoix*, and 1 clove of garlic in a medium saucepan over medium-high heat. Bring to a boil. Lower heat and simmer for about 20 minutes, or until reduced by half. Strain through a fine sieve, discarding solids and reserving liquid in a small saucepan.

Peel and dice potatoes. Place in a medium saucepan with cold water to cover over medium-high heat. Add the remaining 2 cloves of garlic, the onion, and salt to taste and bring to a boil. Lower heat and simmer for about 15 minutes, or until very soft. Drain well. Place in a mixing bowl and, using a potato masher or whip, mash the potatoes until very smooth. Add goat cheese, parsley, and salt and pepper to taste and beat to combine. Cover and set aside.

Lightly flour a baking sheet and set aside.

Using a whisk, beat eggs together. Set aside.

Working with one pasta sheet at a time, cut out 50 circles with a 2-inch round cookie cutter. Tightly cover pasta discs as you work to keep them soft and pliable.

Place 10 discs on a clean, flat surface. Using a pastry brush, generously coat 5 with egg wash. Place a heaping tablespoonful of potato filling in the center of each

A NOTE FROM CHARLIE

I do love potatoes, particularly mashed. I guess that this is what drove me to develop this rather incongruous ravioli filling. Since potatoes are considered peasant food, I thought that the truffle addition would bring them to the king's table.

A NOTE FROM JUDIE

Make sure the mashed potatoes are well drained and firm so you have a stable filling. Don't tell Charlie, but if truffles seem a bit pricey, use a very flavorful wild and meaty mushroom-flavored butter and place paper-thin slices of raw mushroom in the sauce. Extraordinary? No, but delicious nonetheless.

of the egg-washed discs. Cover each with another pasta disc and carefully push the edges together to seal the pasta around the filling. One at a time, pick up ravioli and, using your fingertips, crimp edges together to form a tight seal. Place on prepared baking sheet and let dry in a cool spot (*top left*). Continue making ravioli as above until you have 25 (one extra for the pot!).

Using a truffle slicer or a very sharp paring knife, slice truffle, vertically, into paper-thin slices. Set aside.

Place 2 gallons of water and ⅓ cup coarse salt in a large, deep saucepan or pasta pot. Bring to a boil over high heat.

Return reduced stock to medium heat. Stir in truffle butter and bring to a boil. Turn off heat but leave pan on the burner to keep the stock hot.

Drop half of the ravioli into the boiling water. Cook for 4 minutes, or until tender. Remove ravioli from the boiling water with a wire strainer or slotted spoon. Add remaining ravioli and cook and drain as above. Place 4 ravioli in each of 6 warm, flat soup bowls (*center left*).

While ravioli are cooking, add sliced truffles and chives to the hot stock. Return to a boil. Remove from heat and spoon equal amounts over each ravioli portion (*bottom left*). Serve immediately.

SUGGESTED WINE: A big and buttery Chardonnay, such as Talbott

NOTE: Truffle butter can be purchased by mail order from Zabar's (see page 199) or many other specialty-food stores. It is a wonderful addition to the pantry, as a little will add a lot of flavor to a wide variety of recipes.

Open Ravioli of Seared Salmon and Ratatouille

Serves 6

The flavorful, complex ratatouille serves as a real kicker to the sweet, delicate salmon. All of the components of this dish can be either cooked or seasoned and readied in advance for last-minute preparation.

2 tablespoons ground coriander
Coarse salt
Freshly ground pepper
Six 3-ounce salmon fillets
1 cup Ratatouille juice (see page 64)
2 tablespoons extra-virgin olive oil
2 tablespoons red wine vinegar
1 tablespoon minced fresh basil
2 tablespoons vegetable oil
2 cups Ratatouille (page 64)
Three 12 × S-inch sheets fresh Semolina Pasta (page 191), cut into twelve 4½-inch squares
6 fresh basil leaves

Combine coriander, salt, and pepper and season both sides of the salmon.

Combine ratatouille juice, olive oil, and vinegar in a small saucepan over medium-high heat. Bring to a boil and stir in minced basil. Season to taste with salt and pepper. Turn off heat but leave pan on the burner to keep the vinaigrette hot.

Bring 2 gallons of water to a boil in a large, deep saucepan or pasta pot over high heat. Add salt to taste. Keep on a low boil.

Heat vegetable oil in a large sauté pan until very hot but not smoking. Add the seasoned salmon and sear for about 4 minutes, or until a crisp crust forms. Turn and sear other side for 30 seconds, or until salmon is medium-rare in the center. Place salmon on paper towel–lined baking sheet to drain. Cover and keep warm. Add ratatouille to the sauté pan and stir just to heat through.

Add pasta pieces to the boiling water. Cook for 2 minutes, or until just tender. Using a large strainer, lift pasta pieces from the water. Lay them out, singly, on a paper towel and pat dry. Place one in the center of each of 6 warm plates. Spoon equal portions of ratatouille into the center of each pasta piece.

Place a piece of salmon on top of each. Drop a remaining pasta square on top of each. Spoon warm vinaigrette over all. Garnish with a basil leaf and serve.

A NOTE FROM CHARLIE

Here is a perfect example of using a leftover——the ratatouille juice——to make a scrumptious, well-flavored sauce. The pasta squares make a beautiful presentation (see photograph on page 68), but you could also serve this on pieces of toasted Italian bread.

Spinach Tagliatelle with Seared Scallops and Fresh Sage

Serves 6

This main-course pasta sings with zesty flavor. The cayenne-and-pepper crust infuses a moment of heat that highlights the creaminess of the scallops. Plus. it all comes together in one pan!

18 very large fresh sea scallops
36 large fresh sage leaves
⅓ cup coarse salt plus more to taste
1 ½ tablespoons cayenne pepper
Freshly ground black pepper
5 tablespoons olive oil
¼ cup minced shallots
½ cup dry white wine
1 cup rich Chicken Stock (see Note, page 189)
1 ½ cups julienned carrot
1 cup julienned celery
¼ cup chopped fresh Italian parsley
3 tablespoons unsalted butter
1 ½ pounds fresh Spinach Pasta (see Note, pages 191–192), cut into tagliatelle

Cover a small baking sheet with a clean kitchen towel. If necessary, remove muscles from the scallops. Place scallops on the prepared baking sheet. Pat dry with a paper towel. Cover and refrigerate for at least 30 minutes, or until icy-cold.

Stack 24 of the sage leaves and cut them into a chiffonade. Reserve the chiffonade and the whole leaves separately.

Bring 2 gallons of water and ⅓ cup of salt to a boil over high heat.

Preheat oven to 350°F.

Remove scallops from the refrigerator. Uncover them and generously season with cayenne. black pepper. and salt. Heat 1 tablespoon of oil in a nonstick sauté pan over medium-high heat. When very hot but not smoking. add 9 scallops. Sear for 1½ minutes. Turn and sear the other side for 30 seconds. Place seared scallops in an ovenproof stainless-steel pan. Repeat the process with the remaining scallops. Set aside.

Add 2 tablespoons of oil to the sauté pan. When hot, add the whole sage leaves and fry for 3 minutes, or until crisped but not burned. Remove to paper towels to drain.

Lower heat to medium and stir the shallots into the sage-flavored oil. Sauté for 4 minutes, or until lightly browned. Add the wine and cook over high heat for about

5 minutes, or until pan is almost dry. Add the stock, julienned vegetables, sage chiffonade, parsley, and salt and pepper to taste. Stir in butter and the remaining 2 tablespoons of oil. Lower heat to a very low simmer.

Place pasta in boiling water and cook for 4 to 5 minutes, or until al dente.

While pasta is cooking, place scallops in the preheated oven for 3 to 4 minutes to heat through.

Drain pasta but do not rinse. Immediately add it to the sauce and toss to combine. Mound equal portions onto the center of each of 6 warm plates. Spoon any remaining sauce over the top. Nestle 3 scallops in the center of the pasta and stick 2 sage leaves upright in the center of the scallops. Serve immediately.

SUGGESTED WINE: A Chablis, such as Collet

NOTE: The unique taste of fried sage makes the extra calories well worthwhile. In addition, it adds flavor to the cooking oil you will be using. When frying any herbs for garnish, be sure to save the oil (if not using in the recipe) for use in vinaigrettes or for additional aroma in sautés or grills.

Four-Herb Fettuccine with Green Vegetables and Shaved Asiago

Serves 6

Light, very healthy, and overwhelmingly green, this is a vegetarian's delight. I originally conceived the core of this dish for a vegetarian client's fiftieth birthday. Over the years it has evolved to include other herbs and vegetables. Although I'm sure that it will continue to evolve, the basic rules always remain: Use the best, freshest, greenest compatible herbs and only garden-fresh green vegetables.

2 medium green tomatoes
¾ cup fresh snap peas
1 tightly packed cup trimmed spinach leaves
3 scallions
1 medium zucchini
16 fresh basil leaves
⅓ cup coarse salt plus more to taste
¼ cup extra-virgin olive oil
1 tablespoon Roasted Garlic puree (page 197)
1 ½ cups Vegetable Stock (page 190)
Freshly ground pepper
1 ½ pounds fresh Semolina Pasta (page 191), cut into fettuccine
3 tablespoons chopped fresh chervil
2 tablespoons chopped fresh oregano
2 tablespoons chopped fresh chives
6 ounces Asiago cheese

Place a small pan of water over high heat. Bring to a boil.

Cut an X at the bottom of each tomato. Dip tomatoes in boiling water for 30 seconds, or just until skins have loosened but tomatoes have not softened. Do not turn the heat off. Rinse tomatoes under cold running water. Peel, core, and seed them. Remove membranes and cut tomatoes lengthwise, into ⅛-inch strips. Set aside.

Top and tail the snap peas. Wash them well. Place in boiling water for 30 seconds. Drain and immediately place in an ice-water bath to set texture and color. When chilled, remove from ice bath. Pat dry and set aside.

Wash and dry spinach. Trim off any hard stems. Stack leaves and cut into ¼-inch dice. Set aside.

Trim scallions and wash well. Pat them dry and cut, crosswise on the diagonal, into ½-inch lengths. Set aside.

Wash zucchini. Trim and cut it in half, lengthwise. Holding zucchini together, cut it, crosswise, into ⅛-inch-thick slices. Set aside.

Cut basil leaves into chiffonade. Set aside.

Bring 2 gallons of water and ⅓ cup salt to a boil over high heat.

Heat olive oil in a large sauté pan over medium heat. Add the garlic puree and stir to combine. Stir in snap peas, spinach, scallion, and zucchini and sauté for 2 minutes. Add the stock and tomato and bring to a boil. Lower heat and simmer for 2 minutes. Remove from heat and season to taste with salt and pepper.

Place the pasta in the boiling water and cook for 3½ to 4 minutes, or until al dente. Drain well but do not rinse. Immediately add pasta to the vegetables. Add the basil chiffonade and chopped herbs and toss to combine. Taste and adjust the seasoning with salt and pepper.

Heap equal portions on each of 6 warm dinner plates. Using a cheese shaver or a very sharp knife, shave the cheese over all. Serve immediately.

SUGGESTED WINE: A Sauvignon Blanc, such as Iron Horse

A NOTE FROM CHARLIE

If you want to vary the vegetables for this sauce, select those that require the same amount of cooking time, or blanch some in advance if necessary.

I really like the edge that the sharp Asiago adds when shaved over the pasta. However, you can use whatever grating cheese you like or use none at all!

Crisped Soba Noodle Cake

Makes 6 cakes

I devised this as a base for a sautéed tuna recipe, as I felt it would add so much to the taste and presentation of the dish. The soft noodle interior, flavored with the aromatic sesame, combines with the crisp exterior to make an almost nutlike crunch.

⅓ cup coarse salt plus more to taste
½ cup finely julienned carrot
¼ cup finely julienned celery
½ pound Japanese buckwheat (soba) noodles
2 tablespoons sesame oil
½ tablespoon white pepper or to taste
½ cup all-purpose flour
2 tablespoons toasted sesame seeds
¼ cup canola oil

Bring 2 gallons of water and ⅓ cup of salt to boil in a deep saucepan or pasta pot over high heat. Add the julienned vegetables and cook for 30 seconds, or until just blanched. Do not turn off the flame. Using a strainer, lift out the vegetables and refresh them in an ice-water bath. Pat dry and set aside.

When water returns to a boil, add noodles and cook for 8 minutes, or until just tender. Immediately drain but do not rinse. When well drained, place in a mixing bowl and toss in julienned vegetables, sesame oil, and salt and pepper. Allow to set until cool enough to handle.

Dust a baking sheet with half of the flour and set aside.

Divide noodle mixture into 6 equal portions. Working with one portion at a time, pack it firmly into a 3-inch ring mold (or pastry cutter) to form a solid disc. Place cakes onto prepared baking sheet. When all cakes are formed, sprinkle them with the remaining ¼ cup of flour and coat on all sides with sesame seeds.

Heat canola oil in a large sauté pan over medium heat. Add the noodle cakes and cook for 3 minutes, or until crisp. Turn and cook other side for 2 minutes, or until crisp. Remove from pan and serve immediately.

A NOTE FROM JUDIE

This noodle cake is a great catchall for the savory juices of tuna or any rich, juicy fish, meat, or poultry. These cakes can be molded early in the day and held, covered and refrigerated, until just before you are ready to cook them. Bring them to room temperature before cooking.

Sweet Onion-Risotto Cakes

Serves 6

This is a great side dish to serve with roasted meat or fowl. Unlike my usual "loose" risotto, this should be quite dry so you can easily form it into the cake shape.

5 cups Chicken Stock (page 189)
3 medium white onions
2 tablespoons olive oil
1 ¼ cups Arborio rice
2 tablespoons chopped fresh parsley
2 tablespoons unsalted butter
Coarse salt
Pepper
½ cup fine cornmeal
½ cup all-purpose flour
3 tablespoons vegetable oil

Place the stock in a medium saucepan over medium-high heat. Bring to a boil. Immediately lower heat to just keep stock hot.

Line a baking sheet with sides with waxed paper. Set aside.

Peel the onions and cut them into a fine dice. Heat olive oil in a large, heavy-bottomed saucepan over medium heat. Add the onions and sauté for 5 minutes, or until slightly browned. Add the rice and stir to coat with oil. Add 2 cups of stock and bring to a simmer. Simmer for 20 minutes, adding stock, ½ cup at a time, every 3 minutes, until you have used all of the stock. Stir in parsley and butter. Taste and adjust seasoning with salt and pepper. Pour out into lined pan and smooth top. Set aside to cool.

Place cornmeal on a plate. Set aside.

When rice is cool, divide it into either six or twelve equal portions. Press each portion into a 3-inch ring mold or pastry cutter to form a firm cake. Place cakes in cornmeal to coat each side generously.

Sprinkle flour on a baking sheet and place each cornmeal-coated cake on it.

Heat vegetable oil in a large sauté pan over medium heat. Add the cakes and cook for about 2 minutes per side, or until crisp and golden. Serve hot.

A NOTE FROM JUDIE

You can add some sautéed chopped wild mushrooms, diced potato, or chopped spinach to make these cakes even more interesting. You can mold and coat the cakes early in the day of service. Cover and refrigerate until ready to cook. Bring to room temperature before cooking.

Four-Grain Vegetable Risotto

Serves 6

Here we introduce a variety of nontraditional grains into the very traditional Italian Arborio risotto. I serve this risotto with Seared Chicken Breast with Red Onion Vinaigrette (page 91), but it would work as an accompaniment to almost any meat or poultry dish. It could also be served as an entree, with freshly grated cheese stirred in at the last minute.

¼ cup millet
¼ cup oat groats
¼ cup kasha
¼ cup bulghur wheat
10 cloves garlic, peeled
5 bay leaves
Coarse salt
Freshly ground black pepper
1 medium carrot
1 medium zucchini
1 medium yellow squash
1 medium red bell pepper
3 cups rich Chicken Stock (see Note, page 189)
½ cup (1 stick) unsalted butter
3 tablespoons minced onion
1 cup Arborio rice
2 tablespoons chopped fresh parsley

Separately cook millet, oat groats, kasha, and bulghur wheat in the following manner: Rinse well. Place in a medium saucepan with cold water to cover. Add 2 cloves of garlic, 1 bay leaf, and salt and pepper to taste. Bring to a boil over medium-high heat. Lower heat. Cover and simmer until just tender. The millet and oat groats should take about 25 minutes, and the kasha and bulghur about 15 minutes. Drain off any remaining liquid. Remove the garlic and bay leaf and spread each grain out onto a separate baking sheet to dry.

Preheat oven to 350°F.

For the oat groats only: When dry, place the tray in preheated oven and roast for 15 minutes, or until lightly toasted and very aromatic. Remove from oven. Combine warm groats with all of the other grains in a mixing bowl. Set aside.

Peel and trim the carrot. Trim the zucchini and squash and cut off ¼-inch-thick strips of flesh with skin attached. Set aside the centers for another use, if desired. Core, seed, and remove membrane from the bell pepper. Keeping them separate, cut each vegetable into ¼-inch dice. Bring a small saucepan of salted water to boil over high heat. Separately place each vegetable into a small strainer and dip into the boiling water for 45 seconds, just to set the color and texture. Immediately refresh under cold running water. Pat dry and set aside.

Place chicken stock in a small saucepan over medium-low heat. Bring to a simmer. Lower heat to just keep the stock hot.

Heat 2 tablespoons of butter in a medium saucepan over medium-low heat. Add the onion and sauté for about 5 minutes, or until it has sweated its moisture and is translucent. Stir in the rice, the remaining 2 cloves of garlic, and the remaining bay leaf and sauté for about 5 minutes, or until the rice is glistening. Begin adding the hot chicken stock, ½ cup at a time, stirring constantly and adding additional stock as rice absorbs the previous amount. When last cup of stock has been added, stir in remaining butter and cook, stirring constantly, for about 10 minutes, or until rice is creamy but individual grains are still firm to the tooth. This cooking process should take about 30 minutes. Remove garlic and bay leaf. Fold in the reserved grains and vegetables. Taste and adjust seasoning with salt and pepper. Stir in parsley and serve immediately.

Pumpkin Risotto with Duck Confit and Parmesan

Serves 6

The colors and rich flavors make this an obvious fall dish. The mellow pumpkin, the preserved duck confit, and even the fruitiness of the Riesling help make it a very festive addition to holiday-season entertaining. It is what I call a "loose" risotto, as it is much soupier than the traditional creamy risotto.

½ pound fresh pumpkin
2 medium white onions
2 tablespoons olive oil
1 tablespoon coarse salt plus more to taste
½ tablespoon ground nutmeg
½ tablespoon freshly ground white pepper plus more to taste
¾ cup Riesling wine
3 Duck Confit legs (page 191)
7 cups Chicken Stock (page 189)
5 tablespoons unsalted butter
1 ½ cups Arborio rice
3 tablespoons chopped fresh parsley
½ cup freshly grated Parmesan cheese

Peel and seed pumpkin. Cut it into 1-inch dice and set aside.

Peel onions and cut into ½-inch dice. Divide in half and set aside separately.

Heat oil in a medium saucepan over medium heat. Add the pumpkin, half of the onion, 1 tablespoon salt, nutmeg, and ½ tablespoon white pepper. Cook, stirring frequently, for about 7 minutes, or until pumpkin is tender. Stir in the wine and cook for 15 minutes, stirring occasionally. Remove from heat and allow to cool. When cool, place in a food processor fitted with the metal blade and process until smooth. Scrape from the bowl and set aside.

Remove any skin, bone, sinew, or fat from the duck legs. Pull the meat apart into small pieces. Place in a small saucepan over low heat and allow to just warm. Turn off heat. Cover and leave pan on burner to keep meat warm.

Bring stock to a boil in a medium saucepan over medium heat. Immediately lower heat to just keep stock hot.

Melt 2½ tablespoons butter in a medium, heavy-bottomed saucepan over medium heat. Stir in the rice and remaining onion and cook, stirring with a wooden spoon, for 5 minutes, or until butter begins to brown and onion is translucent. Immediately add about 1½ cups hot stock, or enough just to cover the rice. Simmer gently, stirring occasionally and adding stock, 1 cup at a time, every 3 minutes. After

A NOTE FROM CHARLIE

Don't hesitate to serve this risotto without the duck confit. In fact, if you want to serve it as a first course to be followed by a roast or other meat dish, it might be best standing on its own!

A NOTE FROM JUDIE

You could substitute canned pumpkin or any other sweetly flavored fresh winter squash for the pumpkin and a vegetarian stock for the chicken. Without the confit, this is a delicious vegetarian dish. If using canned pumpkin, sauté the onion in the oil before adding the pumpkin, seasonings, and wine. Cook and puree as directed.

10 minutes, stir in the pumpkin puree and simmer for another 9 minutes, continuing to add stock every 3 minutes. At this point all of the stock should have been used. Add remaining 2½ tablespoons of butter, parsley, and salt and pepper to taste. Cook, stirring constantly, for about 3 minutes, or until butter is completely absorbed. Taste and adjust seasoning.

Spoon equal portions into each of 6 warm, flat soup bowls. Place a mound of duck confit in the center of each serving. Sprinkle some cheese over the top and serve immediately.

SUGGESTED WINE: A dry Riesling, such as Zind-Humbrecht

Israeli Couscous

Israeli couscous is larger grained than the more familiar North African granular semolina. I find that it adds an interesting texture to the plate and certainly piques the diner's curiosity. I like to serve this a bit on the loose side. If there is a delay before serving, you may need additional stock, as the couscous absorbs liquid rapidly as it sits.

1 cup Israeli couscous (see Note)
1 medium onion
2 tablespoons olive oil
2 cups Vegetable Stock (page 190)
Coarse salt
Pepper
3 tablespoons chopped fresh parsley

Place couscous in a large sauté pan over medium heat. Cook, stirring frequently, for about 5 minutes, or until lightly toasted. Remove from heat. Peel and mince onion. Heat olive oil in a medium saucepan over medium heat. Add onion and sauté for about 3 minutes, or until softened. Add couscous and stir to coat. Add stock and bring to a boil. Lower heat. Cover and simmer for about 12 minutes. Season to taste with salt and pepper. Stir in parsley and serve hot.

Vegetable Couscous

This is a simple method of preparing couscous. However, if you have a *couscoussiere*, the steamer pot designed specifically for making traditional couscous dishes, by all means use it. The stock used in the vegetables will add ample flavor to this dish.

1 medium carrot
1 stalk celery
3 cups Chicken Stock (page 189)
1 ½ cups couscous
2 tablespoons olive oil
¼ cup finely diced onion
¼ cup peeled, seeded, and finely diced very ripe tomato
¼ teaspoon cayenne pepper or to taste
1 tablespoon coarse salt or to taste

Peel carrot and cut into a ¼-inch dice. Set aside.

Peel and trim celery. Cut into ¼-inch dice and set aside.

Place 2 cups of stock in a medium saucepan over medium-high heat and bring to a boil. Sift couscous into the stock and stir to combine. Remove from heat. Cover and allow to "bloom" for about 7 minutes.

Heat olive oil in a large sauté pan over medium heat. Add the onion, tomato, and reserved carrot and celery. Cook for about 4 minutes, or until the vegetables have begun to sweat their moisture. Add the remaining cup of stock and season with cayenne and salt to taste. Cook for 4 minutes.

Combine vegetable mixture with couscous and gently stir together. Serve immediately.

A NOTE FROM CHARLIE

I prefer using the medium-grained, quick-cooking couscous rather than the fine-grained instant. I find that it has better flavor and holds its texture longer.

A NOTE FROM JUDIE

You can prepare the couscous and vegetable mixture early in the day. Combine and reheat in a saucepan over low heat or in a preheated 300°F oven just before serving.

Soft Polenta

This polenta is a super base for any dish with a rich sauce. I even like a scoop in the center of a hearty stew.

3 cups Chicken Stock (page 189)
2 tablespoons unsalted butter
Coarse salt
White pepper
1 cup quick-cooking polenta
¼ cup crème fraîche or clabbered cream (see Note)

Place stock in a medium saucepan over medium heat. Bring to a boil. Add butter and salt and pepper to taste. Slowly add polenta, stirring constantly to keep lumps from forming. Lower heat and cook, stirring constantly, for 10 minutes, or until polenta is thickened and cooked. Remove from heat and whip in the crème fraîche or clabbered cream. Season to taste with salt and pepper and serve hot.

IV. AND THEN THERE IS FREE RANGE: POULTRY AND GAME BIRDS

When I was a boy, many of the birds that we ate were either fresh off the farm or caught by my dad, brothers, and me. Nobody told us that our chicken was free range or that the birds we caught were those often destined for fine restaurant tables. We just knew they were delicious. Even though I now deal mostly with farm-raised birds, I can still remember the intense gaminess and rich flavor of the birds of my childhood. It is the memories of these savory tastes that I try to translate to the restaurant kitchen.

Diners, and home cooks, too, are demanding much more than the pale, skinless, boneless chicken breasts, wrapped in clear plastic, stacked in the supermarket poultry section. I'm delighted to be able to satisfy these refined tastes with a wide range of domesticated birds. I use some for their intense flavor, others for texture, and many for their succulent combination of both. I always begin with a whole bird, and I recommend that you do also. Once you make a habit of utilizing all of the parts, breaking down a bird will become an easy and economical part of your kitchen routine. I think that you will also find that your recipe ideas will be challenged by having the extra parts. And, of course, the bones will go right into the stockpot!

If you have not cooked many of the birds in this chapter before, you are going to experience flavors that are delicately gamy, sweet yet intense, and texture that is moist, juicy, and succulent.

The chickens that I use are always the freshest, preservative-free farm-raised birds available. Ranging from the 5- to 10-pound, full-breasted, very flavorful capon to the tiny 1½-pound poussin (or squab chicken), each type of chicken has a place on the plate.

Whichever you use, choose a whole bird, with smooth, blemish-free creamy skin, a plump breast, and full-bodied legs and thighs. The neck and giblets should either be packed in a separate packet, placed in the cleaned bird's cavity, or sold separately. If the chicken is wrapped in clear plastic wrap when purchased, unwrap it when you get home. Thoroughly wash and dry the bird and loosely wrap it in waxed paper. Place it in an airtight container in the coldest part of the refrigerator for no more than two days. Store giblets separately. You can, before storing, break the chicken down to its usable parts and store those you will not be using in the freezer. It is also a good idea to keep an ongoing freezer container to fill with chicken bones to be used for stocks.

Squab (pigeon) is exceptionally tender and juicy. Its delicately flavored dark meat lends itself to all manner of preparations and welcomes rich, complex, and savory flavors. The domesticated pigeon is actually a rock dove, a distant relative of the urban terror we all know so well.

Guinea fowl, also known as *pintade*, is a relative of chicken and partridge, with a dark, faintly gamy meat that requires careful cooking, as it can easily dry out. It is most often braised to hold the moisture in. Guinea hen are more tender than the male birds, but either can be used for any recipe calling for guinea fowl.

I love wild duck—its lean, rich, dark-red meat has such a variety of robust flavors—but because of health concerns we can use only domesticated ducks in the restaurant kitchen. Their flavor is much more uniform, since their diet is not as diverse as that of the wild creatures. Most ducks available today are quite young, weighing no more than 5 pounds. Choose a duck with a wide, full-bodied breast and smooth, taut skin. If fresh duck is not available, purchase a frozen duck and defrost it, refrigerated, for about 36 hours, or until completely thawed.

Farm-raised quail are somewhat milder than wild quail, which are known by a number of other names, depending on the region of the country in which they are eaten. This is particularly confusing in the southern United States, where

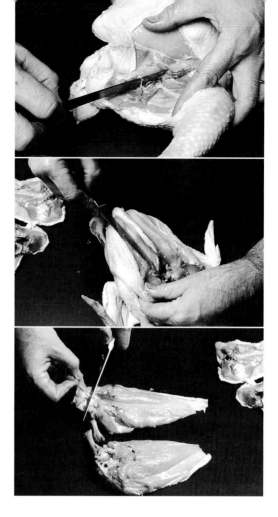

When breaking down poultry, first thoroughly wash and dry the bird. Place the whole bird on a clean cutting board and, using a boning knife, scrape down, against the bone, on either side of the space at the top of the neck crevice (top). This will expose the wishbone, which you can then pull out in one piece.

Cut down into the point between the thigh and the breast and pop the thighbone loose. Using the tip of the knife, trim the meat from along the backbone, taking care to keep the whole "oyster" attached to the thigh meat. If a recipe requires the removal of the thighbone, run your knife along the side of the bone, pushing the meat apart as you cut. Using the tip of the knife, hook under the bone and cut outward (away from your hand) all the way to the end of the joint. Holding the thighbone in your hand, scrape the meat down to the end of the bone and cut through the joint where the thigh joins the drumstick.

Place the knife into the spot where the wing joins the breast. Cut into and up against the inner wingbone, pushing the flesh away from the bone. When the flesh is loose, quickly and carefully snap off the outer wing, leaving a clean, cartilage-free bone handle for the breast.

(continued)

Carefully run the knife down either side of the keelbone to loosen the breasts from the chest cavity (center). Holding on to the wing joint, gently pull the meat away from the bone while running the knife against the bone and cartilage. Hold the carcass down and pull the breast away from it, keeping the meat in one piece. Follow the two bones down to where the wing meets the breast. Cut through the joint, leaving intact the tendon that holds the tenderloin to the breast. Then, using your hand, gently pound down on the knife to cut through. Turn the breast over and flatten it out slightly. Trim off any excess skin and fat from the breast to make a neat package (bottom). You should now have two perfect breasts with handles, two boneless thighs with drumsticks attached, and lots of remnants for the stockpot.

quail are called partridge. Farm-raised quail are available to the home cook both whole and boneless. Their delicately flavored white meat lends itself to a wide variety of preparations, with the boneless particularly well suited to stuffings. They are small and easy to serve in individual portions.

Pheasant, long the king of the nobleman's table, has carried the stigma of strong, almost unpleasant flavor due to "hanging," the centuries-old method of suspending birds in a cool, dry spot to break down the fibers in order to tenderize the meat and intensify the natural gaminess. Since the farm-raised pheasants we now use are naturally tender, juicy, and near honeyed in taste, hanging is no longer necessary.

The slightly gamy flavor of the partridge is a welcome addition to many methods of preparation. The very small, plump-breasted birds have tender white meat that is as tasty roasted as in a stew.

If you can't find any of the game birds, or if they are too expensive, don't hesitate to use chicken in any of the following recipes. The flavors will, of course, be different, but the presentation will be just as interesting and the taste sublime.

Seared Chicken Breast with Red Onion Vinaigrette

Chicken Breast "Saltimbocca" with Sweet Garlic

Alva Double-Garlic Chicken with Overnight Tomatoes

Pan-Roasted Squab with Cabernet-Cassis and Roasted Shallots

Herb-Poached Guinea Fowl in Chanterelle Bouillon

Pepper-Seared Guinea Fowl with New Potato Crêpe

Caramelized Duck Breast with Niçoise Olives and Lemon Confit

Pan-Seared Quail with Sweet Corn and Red Onion Pudding

Sautéed Pheasant with Crisp Spring Roll and Red Onion Marmalade

Roasted Partridge with Morels and Leeks and New Potatoes

Seared Chicken Breast with Red Onion Vinaigrette

Serves 6

This zesty chicken dish is particularly delicious served with Four-Grain Vegetable Risotto (page 80). It then has all the components required to satisfy our current interest in healthier eating.

1 tablespoon plus ½ cup extra-virgin olive oil
1 cup finely diced red onion
2 tablespoons minced fresh thyme
Coarse salt
Freshly ground black pepper
2 cups Chicken Stock (page 189)
¾ cup red Burgundy
3 tablespoons canned tomato puree
2 cloves garlic
1 Sachet (page 197)
3 tablespoons red wine vinegar
3 whole boneless chicken breasts, skin on
3 tablespoons coarsely cracked black pepper
1 tablespoon corn oil

Place 1 tablespoon of olive oil in a small sauté pan over medium heat. When hot, add the onion. Sauté for 10 minutes, or until the onion is well browned and caramelized. Stir in thyme and salt and pepper to taste. Set aside.

Combine stock, wine, tomato puree, garlic, and sachet in a medium saucepan over medium-high heat. Bring to a boil. Lower heat and simmer for about 25 minutes, or until liquid is reduced to ¾ cup. Remove from heat. Discard sachet and pour liquid into a heatproof bowl. Allow to rest for 10 minutes, or until slightly cooled. Then alternately whisk in ½ cup of olive oil and vinegar until just emulsified. Stir in caramelized onion. Keep warm in the top half of a double boiler over hot water until ready to serve.

Preheat oven to 375°F.

Split chicken breasts in half and trim off any cartilage or bone. Generously season with salt and cracked pepper. Heat corn oil in a large, ovenproof sauté pan over medium-high heat. When hot, add chicken breasts, skin-side down. Cook for 5 minutes, or until golden-brown. Turn breasts, place entire pan in preheated oven, and roast for 8 to 10 minutes, or until cooked through and golden-brown. Remove from oven and place over low heat. Add the vinaigrette and baste to coat. When well coated, serve with vinaigrette spooned over the top.

SUGGESTED WINE: A full-bodied red wine, such as a Guigal Gigondas

A NOTE FROM JUDIE

This chicken with red wine vinaigrette has its genesis in the traditional French *coq au vin*, chicken stewed in a hearty wine sauce. Charlie's lighter version quick-cooks the chicken, and the red wine is used in a warm vinaigrette to add flavor and depth.

Chicken Breast "Saltimbocca" with Sweet Garlic

Serves 6

In the Roman fashion, saltimbocca is usually made with veal. Traditionally, a veal scallop is sprinkled with chopped fresh sage, topped with prosciutto, and then sautéed in butter and finished in a white-wine braise. If you wish, my version could also be made with veal or even turkey scallops.

2 ½ to 3 pounds mixed hearty greens, such as mustard, beet, or chard (see Note)
Coarse salt
18 fingerling potatoes (see Note)
12 cloves Roasted Garlic (page 197)
Six 6-ounce boneless, skinless chicken breast halves
12 fresh sage leaves
6 slices prosciutto
2 tablespoons vegetable oil
2 teaspoons cracked black pepper
3 tablespoons minced shallots
½ cup finely diced, peeled, and seeded tomatoes
3 ½ cups Chicken Stock (page 189)
2 tablespoons olive oil
Freshly ground black pepper
3 tablespoons unsalted butter
3 tablespoons roughly chopped fresh Italian parsley

A NOTE FROM BOTH OF US

Try to combine greens of compatible colors and shapes. A hint of red from beet or red chard adds interest to other greens.

If you can't find fingerling potatoes, use the smallest new potatoes available.

Wash and dry greens. Place them in boiling, salted water for 2 minutes, or until just tender but still bright green. Drain and place in an ice-water bath to stop cooking and set the color. Drain and pat dry. Lay in a clean kitchen towel. Fold ends in and tightly twist to squeeze out all moisture. Remove from towel and roughly chop. Set aside.

Wash potatoes. Place them in salted water to cover in a medium saucepan over high heat. Bring to a boil. Lower heat and simmer for about 10 minutes, or until just tender. Drain and place in an ice-water bath to stop cooking. Drain and pat dry. Set aside.

Remove garlic from the skins and set aside.

Trim chicken of any fat or sinew. Place 2 sage leaves in the center of each breast half. Wrap a slice of prosciutto around the center of each breast, slightly overlapping the edges to seal. Using kitchen twine, tie the prosciutto in place.

Preheat oven to 150°F.

Heat vegetable oil in a large, nonstick sauté pan over medium heat. Season chicken breasts with cracked pepper and lay in the pan. Cook, turning occasionally, for about 12 minutes, or until breasts are well browned on all sides. Remove to a heatproof platter and lightly cover with aluminum foil. Place in the preheated oven to keep warm.

Return sauté pan to medium heat. Add shallots and sauté for 1 minute. Stir in the tomato and reserved garlic and sauté for 2 minutes. Add the stock and cook, stirring occasionally, for about 5 minutes, or until reduced by half.

While sauce is reducing, heat olive oil in another large sauté pan over medium heat. Add the greens and potatoes and toss to combine. Season to taste with salt and pepper and cook for 2 minutes, or until very hot. Remove from heat.

Whisk butter and parsley into reduced sauce. Taste and adjust seasoning with salt and pepper. Lower heat and keep warm.

Place an equal portion of greens in the center of each of 6 warm plates. Place an equal number of potatoes around the edge. Remove chicken from oven, clip and remove twine, and place a breast on top of each mound of greens. (If any juices have run onto the platter, pour them into the sauce and whisk to combine.)

Spoon equal portions of sauce over the top of each chicken breast. Grind some fresh pepper over each plate and serve immediately.

SUGGESTED WINE: A Barbaresco, such as that from Roagna

Alva Double-Garlic Chicken
with Overnight Tomatoes

Serves 6

The pungent garlic flavors become dense and sweet in this simple dish created for my bistro-style restaurant, Alva. The oven-dried tomatoes can be made a few days in advance and stored, airtight, at room temperature.

12 ripe plum tomatoes
Coarse salt
Pepper
3 large bulbs garlic
¼ cup olive oil
3 large, whole chicken breasts with wings attached
6 chicken thighs
2 large bunches arugula
1 ½ pounds fresh spinach
3 tablespoons corn oil
3 cups Chicken Stock (page 189)
3 tablespoons unsalted butter
3 tablespoons chopped fresh Italian parsley
6 sprigs fresh parsley

Preheat oven to 350°F.

Wash and dry tomatoes. Cut them in half, lengthwise, and season to taste with salt and pepper. Place on a wire rack on a small baking sheet in preheated oven. Lower heat to 175°F and roast for 8 hours, or until almost completely dry. Remove from oven and set aside.

Raise oven heat to 325°F.

Separate cloves from garlic bulbs. Toss cloves in 2 tablespoons of olive oil. Place them on a small baking dish in preheated oven and roast for 18 minutes, or until very soft. Peel each clove and divide the peeled cloves in half. Puree and reserve one half. Set remaining half aside.

Cut and bone chicken breasts as directed on page 89–90. Pat dry. Using a boning knife, carefully cut down into the thighbones. Cut against the bones to detach the meat from the bones. Lift meat away from bones. Trim off any cartilage or excess fat. Pat dry.

Rub garlic puree into the skin of all chicken pieces. Season to taste with salt and pepper.

Wash and dry arugula and spinach well. Set aside.

Heat 1½ tablespoons of corn oil in each of 2 large sauté pans over medium heat. Add the chicken, skin-side down. Tilting the pans from time to time to distribute the fat evenly, cook for 10 minutes, or until skin is golden-brown and crusty. Turn and cook for 8 minutes, or until chicken is golden-brown and just cooked through, draining pan if excess fat builds up. Remove chicken from pan and drain on paper towels. Cover lightly and keep warm.

Return both pans to medium heat. Place stock, reserved whole garlic cloves, butter, and parsley in one pan. Raise heat and cook for 5 minutes, or until slightly thickened. Place arugula and spinach in the remaining pan, adding no more than 2 tablespoons of olive oil, if necessary, to coat the greens lightly. Sauté for 3 minutes, or until just softened. Taste and adjust seasoning in both pans with salt and pepper. Add tomatoes to sauce and simmer for 30 seconds.

Place greens in the center of a warm platter. Slightly overlap the chicken pieces, alternating a breast and a thigh, around the edge of the bed of greens. Spoon sauce over the chicken, placing a tomato on top of each chicken piece. Garnish with parsley sprigs and serve immediately.

SUGGESTED WINE: A Pinot Noir, such as Au Bon Climat

Pan-Roasted Squab with Cabernet-Cassis and Roasted Shallots

Serves 6

The cassis is a European black currant generally used to make syrup or liqueur. Slightly tart with a rich color, it combines well with the full-bodied, fruity Cabernet wine. Veal stock rather than chicken is called for in this recipe to highlight the delicately flavored dark meat of the squab.

Six 1 ¼-pound squabs
½ cup dried black currants
6 tablespoons olive oil
2 cups Mirepoix *(page 197)*
3 cloves garlic, peeled
3 cups Cabernet Sauvignon
6 large sprigs fresh thyme
4 ½ cups Veal Stock (page 189)
12 large shallots
Coarse salt
Pepper
2 tablespoons chopped fresh Italian parsley
1 recipe Vegetable Couscous (page 85)

Wash and dry squabs. Cut, as directed on page 89–90, into 6 full breasts with wing handles and 12 legs with boneless thighs. Trim off any fat, cartilage, and membrane from the breasts and leg/thigh pieces. Pat dry and set aside. Using a cleaver or heavy French knife, chop squab carcasses into 2- to 3-inch pieces and set aside.

Place currants in a small heatproof bowl. Cover with boiling water and allow to rest for about 30 minutes, or until well plumped. Drain well and cover to keep softened until ready to use.

Preheat oven to 375°F.

Heat a roasting pan in preheated oven. Add 2 tablespoons of olive oil and the carcass pieces. Roast, turning from time to time, for 15 minutes. Add the *mirepoix* and garlic and roast for an additional 25 minutes, or until bones are well browned. Remove from oven and place over medium heat. Add wine, stirring constantly to deglaze the pan. Scrape into a large saucepan. Add thyme and place over medium-high heat. Cook for about 20 minutes, or until pan is almost dry. Add the stock and bring to a simmer. Lower heat and simmer for about 40 minutes, or until reduced by half. Remove from heat and strain through a fine sieve into a medium saucepan. Discard solids. Set saucepan aside.

Preheat oven to 350°F.

Toss shallots and 2 tablespoons of olive oil on a small baking pan. When shallots are well coated, place them in preheated oven and roast for 20 minutes, or until very soft. Remove from oven and allow to set until just cool enough to handle. Using kitchen shears or a very sharp knife, snip off the top end of each shallot and peel back the skin, leaving the tender, whole shallot. Place in a small pan and cover lightly. Keep warm until ready to use.

Lower oven temperature to 300°F.

Line a baking sheet with paper towels. Set aside.

Heat the remaining 2 tablespoons of olive oil in a large sauté pan over high heat. Season squab pieces with salt and pepper. Place legs, skin-side down, in the hot pan. Sear for 4 minutes, or until golden. Turn and cook for 4 minutes. Transfer to an ovenproof pan and place in preheated oven. Place breast pieces, skin-side down, in the sauté pan. Sear for 6 minutes, or until golden. Turn and cook for 2 minutes, or until still blush-red in the center and slightly tight to the fingertip touch. Remove and drain on prepared baking sheet. Remove leg pieces from the oven and place them on baking sheet to drain.

Place sauce over medium heat. Add currants and parsley and bring to a boil. Season to taste with salt and pepper. Remove from heat.

Place equal portions of vegetable couscous in the center of each of 6 warm plates. Place a whole squab breast and 2 legs against the couscous. Spoon sauce over the top and nestle two shallots between the squab pieces. Serve immediately.

SUGGESTED WINE: A deep Cabernet, such as Sterling or Silver Oak

Herb-Poached Guinea Fowl in Chanterelle Bouillon

Serves 6

This is a wonderfully light but luxurious late-supper dish served with a great crusty bread, a light green salad, and a glass of light red wine.

1 pound fresh chanterelles
2 small turnips
2 medium carrots
½ pound celery root
6 small shallots
3 cloves garlic
Three 2½-pound guinea fowl
Coarse salt
Pepper
2 tablespoons safflower oil
1 Sachet (page 197)
3 tablespoons each minced fresh tarragon, chervil, and chives

Brush chanterelles clean of debris. If they are large, cut in half. Set aside.

Peel and trim turnips, carrots, and celery root. Cut turnips into 6 even wedges. Cut carrots, crosswise, into ½-inch-thick discs. Cut celery root into ½-inch dice. Peel shallots and garlic. Set aside.

Wash and dry guinea fowl. Season to taste with salt and pepper.

Heat oil in a large sauté pan over medium heat. Add the guinea fowl and cook, turning frequently, until browned on all sides. Remove from pan and set aside. Return pan to medium heat and add reserved mushrooms. Sauté for 4 minutes. Remove mushrooms from pan and set aside. Place guinea fowl in a large Dutch oven. Add water to just cover along with the sachet and the reserved turnips, carrots, celery root, shallots, and garlic. Place over medium-high heat and bring to a simmer. Simmer for 5 minutes, skimming off all fat and impurities that rise to the top. Continue to simmer for 20 minutes, or until vegetables are very soft. Carefully remove birds to a platter. With a slotted spoon, lift out vegetables and place in a bowl. Discard garlic and sachet. Return liquid to a simmer. Add reserved mushrooms and bring to a boil. Lower heat and simmer for 15 minutes, or until liquid is reduced by half. Skim any fat and impurities from the top. Taste and adjust the seasoning with salt and pepper.

With a sharp knife, cut the birds into serving pieces, using just the breasts and legs with thighs attached. Return to the hot broth. Add the reserved cooked vegetables and the herbs. Bring to a boil. Immediately remove from heat. Place 1 breast half and 1 leg/thigh in each of 6 warm, shallow soup plates. Ladle broth and vegetables into the bowl and serve immediately (see photograph on page 88).

A NOTE FROM JUDIE

If you can't find chanterelles and guinea fowl, this recipe tastes almost as good using small chickens and any mushroom you can find, even supermarket button mushrooms.

Pepper-Seared Guinea Fowl
with New Potato Crêpe

Serves 6

This is a wonderful dish to welcome fall. Rich in flavor, guinea fowl offers a mellow introduction to game birds. A relative of partridge, it can be used interchangeably with chicken in most recipes.

3 guinea fowl
1 cup dry white wine
5 tablespoons olive oil
1 ½ cups Mirepoix *(page 197)*
1 Sachet *(page 197)*
4 cups Chicken Stock *(page 189)*
Coarse salt
Cracked black pepper
6 Red Bliss potatoes
1 large Spanish onion
3 tablespoons chopped fresh parsley
Six 8-inch Crêpes *(page 196)*
Approximately 3 tablespoons melted unsalted butter or Clarified Butter *(page 197)*
1 tablespoon vegetable oil
1 tablespoon unsalted butter
1 ½ cups sliced morels (or other well-flavored wild mushrooms)
6 sprigs fresh parsley

Using a sharp boning knife, remove each breast half from the guinea fowl and cut as directed on pages 89–90 into 6 boneless breasts with wing handles. Do not remove the skin. Cover breasts and refrigerate until ready to roast.

Again using the boning knife, cut down through the leg joint, removing all 6 legs from the fowl. Carefully remove skin, fat, and tendons. Make a deep cut, lengthwise, down each leg and scrape the meat away from the bone. Cut the leg meat into strips 2 inches long by ¼ inch thick. Cover and refrigerate.

Preheat oven to 350°F.

Place guinea carcasses in a roasting pan in preheated oven and roast for 40 minutes, or until golden brown. Remove from oven. Drain off all fat. Using a cleaver, crack carcasses into small pieces and set aside.

Place roasting pan over medium-high heat. Add wine and cook, stirring constantly, for about 3 minutes to deglaze pan. Scrape mixture from the pan and reserve.

Heat 1 tablespoon of olive oil in a large saucepan over medium heat. Add the *mirepoix* and sachet and sauté for 3 minutes. Add the reserved roasted guinea bones and wine and cook for 10 minutes. Raise heat and add 3 cups of chicken stock. Season to taste with salt and pepper. Bring to a boil. Lower heat and simmer for 30 minutes. Remove from heat and strain through a fine sieve into a clean saucepan. Skim all fat and any particles from the top. Return to medium heat and cook for about 15 minutes, or until reduced to 1½ cups. Remove from heat and set aside.

Peel potatoes. Place them in a medium saucepan with water to cover over medium-high heat. Add salt to taste. Bring to a boil. Lower heat and simmer for 12 minutes, or until potatoes are tender when pierced with the point of a sharp knife. Drain well. Cut, crosswise, into thin slices. Set aside.

Peel onion and slice it, crosswise, into thin slices. Set aside.

Remove leg meat from the refrigerator. Season lightly with salt and pepper to taste. Heat 2 tablespoons of olive oil in a medium sauté pan over medium heat. When very hot but not smoking, add the meat and sauté for 4 minutes. Stir in the remaining cup of stock and cook for about 15 minutes, or until meat is very tender and the liquid has reduced to a glaze. Remove from heat and scrape into a mixing bowl.

Heat remaining 2 tablespoons of oil in the same sauté pan over medium heat. Add onion and sauté for 5 minutes, or until lightly browned. Stir in potatoes and sauté for 1 minute. Remove from heat and add to meat. Stir in 1 tablespoon of chopped parsley. Taste and adjust seasoning with salt and pepper.

Lay the crêpes out on a clean, flat surface. Using a pastry brush, lightly coat one side with melted butter. Divide potato stuffing into 6 equal portions and place a portion in the center of each crêpe. Fold the sides of the crêpes over the filling. Starting from one open end, roll up each crêpe to make a firm but not tight cylinder. Again, brush them with melted butter. Place on a small nonstick baking sheet and set aside.

Preheat oven to 300°F.

Remove breasts from refrigerator. Season generously with coarse salt and cracked pepper. Heat vegetable oil in a sauté pan large enough to hold the 6 breasts over medium-high heat. When very hot, place the breasts, skin-side down, in pan. Sear for 5 minutes, or until lightly browned. Turn and cook for 4 minutes. Remove to a baking sheet and place in the preheated oven along with the crêpes. Bake for about 10 minutes, or until meat is just cooked and crêpes are golden.

Melt the tablespoon of butter in the same sauté pan over medium heat, stirring constantly to scrape up solids from the bottom of the pan. Add morels and sauté for 6 minutes, or until tender. Add reduced stock, remaining 2 tablespoons of chopped parsley, and salt and pepper to taste. Bring to a simmer and cook for 2 minutes. Taste and adjust seasoning. Reduce heat to very low to keep sauce warm.

Remove crêpes and breasts from oven. Lay one crêpe in the center of each of 6 warm dinner plates. Angle a breast against each crêpe. Spoon a generous portion of sauce over the crêpe and fowl. Garnish with a sprig of fresh parsley and serve immediately.

SUGGESTED WINE: A medium-bodied Cabernet, such as Jordan Vineyards

Caramelized Duck Breast with Niçoise Olives and Lemon Confit

Serves 6

You might want to serve this duck over a steamed grain such as couscous, or even mashed white or sweet potatoes, or, better yet, accompanied by Butternut Squash Flan (see page 66).

2 pounds duck bones
1 ½ cups red wine
2 cups Mirepoix *(page 197)*
1 Sachet *(page 197)*
2 cups Chicken Stock *(page 189)*
2 cups Veal Stock *(page 189)*
6 large boneless duck breasts, *skin on*
Coarse salt
Pepper
½ cup sliced, pitted Niçoise olives
¼ cup Lemon Confit *(page 191)*
3 tablespoons minced shallots
2 tablespoons chopped fresh Italian parsley
¼ cup Tomato Oil *(optional; see page 196)*
6 sprigs fresh Italian parsley

Preheat oven to 375°F.

Cut bones into 2-inch pieces. Place them in a small roasting pan in preheated oven and roast, stirring occasionally, for 30 minutes, or until well browned. Remove from oven and place the pan over medium heat. Add ½ cup red wine and cook, stirring constantly, for 3 minutes, or until pan is deglazed and liquid has evaporated. Scrape into a medium saucepan. Add *mirepoix* and sauté for 4 minutes. Stir in remaining cup of wine and sachet and cook for 5 minutes. Add stocks and bring to a boil. Lower heat and simmer for 45 minutes, or until liquid is reduced to 1½ cups. Remove from heat and strain through a fine sieve into a small bowl. Set aside.

Season duck breasts with salt and pepper. Heat a large, heavy skillet over medium heat. When very hot but not smoking, add breasts, skin-side down. Cook, draining off excess fat from time to time, for 14 minutes, or until most of the fat is rendered out and skin is nicely browned and crisp. Turn and cook for 3 minutes, or until meat is cooked to medium and still moist in the center. Remove to a warm platter. Cover lightly and keep warm.

Drain any excess fat from the skillet. Place over medium heat and add olives, confit, and shallots, stirring constantly to bring up any bits of meat stuck to the bot-

A NOTE FROM JUDIE

All domestic ducks raised in the United States today are the descendants of either Mallard or Muscovy ducks. The best known of these is the large-breasted Long Island duck, also known as Peking duck because it is the progeny of a drake and 3 hens that arrived on a clipper ship from China in the late 1800s.

A NOTE FROM CHARLIE

Since you will be cutting the breasts from whole ducks, use the legs for confit, the bits and pieces of leftover meat in hors d'oeuvres or appetizers, and the bones for stocks and sauces.

tom of the pan. Stir in reserved sauce and cook. stirring frequently. for 5 minutes. Taste and adjust seasoning with salt and pepper. Stir in the chopped parsley and remove from heat.

Using a very sharp knife. cut the duck breasts on the bias into thin slices. Arrange one breast. slightly fanned. in the center of each of 6 warm plates. Spoon equal portions of sauce over the top. If using. drizzle some tomato oil around the perimeter of each plate and garnish with a parsley sprig. Serve immediately.

SUGGESTED WINE: A fruity red wine. such as Ridge Zinfandel

Pan-Seared Quail with Sweet Corn and Red Onion Pudding

Serves 6

Beautiful colors contrast on the plate to make this an especially appealing dinner-party recipe. Much can be done in advance, which allows the cook to enjoy the guests and the meal!

Twelve 6-ounce quail
3 tablespoons corn oil
2 cups Mirepoix *(page 197)*
1 cup white wine
3 cups Chicken Stock (page 189)
1 cup Veal Stock (page 189)
8 peppercorns
2 large red onions
3 tablespoons olive oil
¼ cup minced fresh thyme
Coarse salt
Pepper
½ pound fresh haricots verts *or tiny green beans*
2 cups Savory Corn Cake batter (page 17)
2 tablespoons minced fresh Italian parsley
6 sprigs fresh thyme

Debone quail breasts as directed on page 89–90, leaving the wing-joint handle. Remove legs and thighs at the point where the thigh meets the body, as directed on page 89. Wash quail pieces and pat them dry. Cover and refrigerate until ready to use.

Chop carcasses and wing parts into small pieces. Place in a large saucepan over medium heat. Stir in 1 tablespoon of corn oil and the *mirepoix*. Sauté for 5 minutes, or until bones and vegetables are beginning to brown. Stir in wine and cook, stirring constantly, for 2 minutes, or until pan is deglazed. Simmer for 5 minutes, or until wine has almost evaporated and pan is almost dry. Add stocks and peppercorns and bring to a boil. Lower heat and simmer for 20 minutes, or until liquid is reduced to 2 cups. Remove from heat and strain through a fine sieve into a small bowl, discarding the solids. Set aside.

Line 2 baking sheets with clean kitchen towels. Set aside.

Peel and trim onions. Cut them, crosswise, into ¼-inch-thick slices. Heat 2 tablespoons of olive oil in a large sauté pan over medium heat. Add onion slices and cook, stirring frequently, for 4 minutes, or until onions are soft. Stir in 2 tablespoons of thyme and lightly season with salt and pepper. Remove from heat and place on one of the prepared baking sheets to drain.

Trim beans of stem ends. Wash them well. Place in boiling salted water to cover for 1 minute, or until color is set and beans are crisp-tender. Drain and refresh under cold running water. Pat dry and set aside.

Preheat oven to 350°F.

Generously grease six 5-ounce molds (see Note). Pour enough of the corn cake batter into each mold to cover the bottom generously. Next, place a layer of red onion. Then continue to add alternating layers of batter and onions until the molds are three-quarters full. Place in preheated oven and bake for 20 minutes, or until tops are golden and a toothpick, inserted in the center, comes out clean.

While pudding is cooking, heat remaining 2 tablespoons of corn oil in a large sauté pan over medium heat. Remove quail from refrigerator and season legs with salt and pepper. Place legs in the pan, skin-side down, and sear for 3 minutes, or until golden. Turn and sear for 2 minutes. Remove from pan and place on remaining towel-lined pan to drain. Immediately season breasts with salt and pepper to taste and add, skin-side down, to the hot pan. Sear for 3 minutes, or until golden. Turn and sear for 1 minute. Remove and place in the pan with the legs.

Carefully wipe any oil from pan with a paper towel. Return to medium-high heat. Add reserved sauce, parsley, and remaining thyme. Bring to a boil. Lower heat and simmer for 5 minutes, or until sauce has reduced to 1½ cups. Taste and adjust seasoning with salt and pepper.

Heat the remaining tablespoon of olive oil in a small sauté pan over medium heat. Add reserved beans and sauté for 1 minute, or until just heated through. Place equal portions in the center of each of 6 warm plates. Arrange 4 quail legs and 4 breasts in a star form around the beans. Unmold a pudding between the quail pieces. Spoon sauce over the quail and garnish with a thyme sprig. Serve immediately.

SUGGESTED WINE: A light, well-balanced Pinet Noir, such as Etude

Sautéed Pheasant with Crisp Spring Rolls and Red Onion Marmalade

Serves 6

The spring roll is certainly a somewhat plebeian approach to pheasant but one that, I think, makes an appealing addition to the plate. The filling will make enough for about twelve spring rolls, so make up the extra and freeze them for later use.

Three 3-pound pheasants
¼ head Savoy cabbage
2 tablespoons sesame oil
Coarse salt
Pepper
1 tablespoon minced fresh ginger
½ cup julienned carrot
½ cup julienned celery
½ cup julienned leek
¼ cup all-purpose flour
Six 8-inch square wheat-flour egg-roll wrappers
2 large eggs
4 cups plus 2 tablespoons corn oil
2 cloves garlic, peeled
¼ cup minced shallots
1 cup white wine
3 tablespoons rice wine vinegar
3 cups Veal Stock (page 189)
2 tablespoons unsalted butter
⅛ teaspoon cayenne pepper or to taste
2 tablespoons minced fresh Italian parsley
6 tablespoons Spicy Red Onion Marmalade (page 195)

Break down the pheasants as directed on page 89–90, leaving the breasts with the wing-joint handles and separating the legs from the thighs. Debone legs and thighs. Remove skin and cut meat into thin julienne. Refrigerate breasts until ready to use.

Cut cabbage into chiffonade. Set aside.

Heat a large, nonstick sauté pan over medium heat. Add the julienned pheasant meat and sesame oil. Season to taste with salt and pepper and sauté for 4 minutes. Add the ginger and the julienned vegetables and sauté for 2 minutes. Add the cabbage and cook, stirring frequently, for 10 minutes, or until vegetables are tender but still firm. Taste and adjust seasoning with salt and pepper. Remove from heat and scrape onto a baking sheet to cool.

(continued)

Sprinkle flour on a baking sheet. Set aside.

When the filling is cool, lay egg-roll wrappers, singly, on a clean, damp kitchen towel to make them pliable.

Beat the eggs with 1 tablespoon of cold water. Using a pastry brush, apply egg wash generously in a 1-inch edge around each egg-roll wrapper. Working with one wrapper at a time, place a mound of filling in the center. Fold one corner over the filling. Roll halfway, then fold the opposing corners over the roll and continue rolling to make a firm cylinder. Seal the final corner onto the cylinder with a bit of egg wash. Place on floured pan as you continue to make rolls.

Preheat oven to 400°F.

Heat 2 tablespoons of corn oil in a large sauté pan over medium heat. Rub each pheasant breast with garlic and season to taste with salt and pepper. Lay, skin-side down, in the pan. Sear, shaking the pan from time to time to distribute oil, for 8 minutes, or until skin is crisp and golden. Place on a baking sheet in preheated oven and roast for 8 minutes, or until meat is firm to the touch.

While breasts are roasting, return sauté pan to medium heat after discarding any excess oil. Add shallots and sauté for 3 minutes. Stir in wine and vinegar and cook for 2 minutes. Add the stock, butter, and cayenne and cook for about 10 minutes, or until mixture is reduced to a saucelike consistency. Taste and adjust seasoning with salt.

While breasts are roasting and sauce is reducing, heat remaining 4 cups of corn oil in a deep-fryer (or deep-sided saucepan) over high heat to 350°F on a candy thermometer. Fry 3 spring rolls at a time for 3 minutes, or until golden and crisp. Drain on paper towels. When ready to serve, cut through the center, on the bias. Place one half in the center of each of 6 warm plates. Lean a breast against it. Stand the remaining half next to the breast. Stir the parsley into the sauce and spoon over the top of the pheasant and around the edge of the plate. Place a tablespoon of red onion marmalade on each plate. Serve immediately.

SUGGESTED WINE: A big, full-bodied Pinot Noir, such as Beaux Frères

Roasted Partridge with Morels and Leeks and New Potatoes

Serves 6

Although I have used partridge, this recipe can be adapted to any other bird, even chicken. Whatever bird you use, remember to keep it moist and juicy, even erring on the side of undercooking before carving, as it will finish cooking when returned to the oven.

Six 1½-pound partridges
Six 1 × 2-inch pieces lemon zest
6 sprigs fresh tarragon
3 tablespoons corn oil
2 cups Mirepoix (page 197)
Coarse salt
Pepper
4 cups Chicken Stock (page 189)
1 cup white wine
2 tablespoons unsalted butter
3 tablespoons minced shallots
24 large fresh morels (see Note)
½ cup diced fresh spinach leaves
1 recipe Leeks and New Potatoes (see page 63)

Preheat oven to 500°F.

Wash and dry partridges. Trim off outer wing joints and prepare the wing handles as directed on page 89–90. Using a paper towel, pat cavities completely dry. Place a piece of lemon zest and a tarragon sprig in the cavity of each bird. Using kitchen twine, tie the legs to the body to close the cavities and help the birds keep their shape. Set aside.

Heat 1 tablespoon of oil in a large sauté pan over medium heat. Add the *mirepoix* and sauté for 4 minutes, or until just softened. Scrape into a roasting pan large enough to hold the 6 birds. Add the wing scraps and neck and set aside.

Wipe the sauté pan clean. Return to medium heat and add the remaining 2 tablespoons of oil. Season partridge with salt and pepper to taste. Place birds in the pan, two at a time, and sear for about 4 minutes, turning frequently until all sides are browned. As the birds are browned, place them, breast-side up, on the *mirepoix* in the roasting pan. When all birds are browned, place roasting pan in preheated oven and roast for 12 minutes, or until skin is golden. Remove from oven and place birds on a warm platter. Cover lightly to keep warm. Turn oven down to 275°F.

Place roasting pan over high heat. Add the stock and wine and, stirring constantly, bring to a boil. Lower heat and simmer for 10 minutes. Remove from heat

A NOTE FROM JUDIE

If you can't find fresh morels, use dry ones. Just make sure to reconstitute them in hot water (or hot stock) to cover before adding them to the sauce.

and strain through a fine sieve, pressing on the solids to extract the juices. Reserve liquid and discard the solids.

Carve the partridges, removing each breast half in one piece. Cover lightly and keep warm.

Carefully carve the meat from the thighs and legs. If still too rare, place on a small, nonstick baking sheet and return to the oven to finish cooking.

Heat butter in a medium sauté pan over medium heat. Add the shallots and sauté for 2 minutes. Add the morels and sauté for 2 minutes. Stir in reserved sauce and simmer for 5 minutes. Stir in spinach and season to taste with salt and pepper.

Place a small mound of leeks and new potatoes in the center of each of 6 warm plates. Place 2 large pieces of thigh/leg meat on top of them. Lean 2 breast halves up against each leek and new potato mound. Spoon equal portions of the sauce and morels over the top and around the plate. Serve immediately.

SUGGESTED WINE: A rich, earthy Merlot, such as a Ravenswood

V. AT HOME ON THE RANGE:
MEAT AND GAME

To me, meat is not only the backbone of the kitchen, it is its soul. It stars as the center of the meal, and it provides the stocks and broths upon which most of the great sauces are built, as well as many of the heartwarming soups and stews that can feed the multitudes and nourish the spirit. It is not without pith that the French word for meat, *viande*, is derived from the Latin *vivenda*, meaning "that which maintains life."

I am stalwart in my support of meat as the main feature of the menu. As much as it seems that lighter meals are the rule nowadays, I find that restaurant diners appreciate the luxury of the enjoyment of a variety of meats. And although fat is the conductor of flavor through all meat, today's leaner cuts provide more than enough flavor with fewer calories. Using only the highest grade, we butcher our meats to highlight their texture and ensure rich savor. If you use a fine-quality butcher, these characteristics will be the base of your meat recipes also.

In the traditional cook's language, there are three types of meat: white (veal, pork, rabbit); red (beef, lamb); and dark (game). Offal, the edible internal organs and other parts as well as some edible external pieces of all animals, is also divided into white and

red, with sweetbreads and marrow being the outstanding whites, and liver, kidneys, and tongue among the red. All meats are a terrific source of protein, mineral salts, and vitamins, but since they are also high in saturated fats and cholesterol, it is generally recommended that they not be eaten daily. Since nothing provides a feeling of culinary fulfillment as does a well-cooked piece of meat, the occasional indulgence becomes even more pleasurable.

When purchasing meats, always use a premium butcher who deals in prime meats. This is your best insurance of fine quality. Each type should retain a clear, clean color.

Beef should be a bright, almost shiny red with a fine webbing of fat; veal a fair, warm pink with very pure white fat; lamb rosy, deep pink, and pork an almost white pink. The flavor will be manipulated in the cooking: Tender, prime-quality meats require minimal cooking, as overcooking will toughen them, while lesser grades of meat will become tender and delicious with long periods of braising.

Celebrations call for meals for the heart and soul. It is this reason that meats, to me, symbolize *feasts*. For those of us who take pleasure in the rituals of the table, the smell and taste of finely prepared meats call for the napkin under the chin, a decanter of a great Bordeaux or Cabernet, and the company of good friends. As I said, the backbone and soul of the kitchen!

Sautéed Veal Medallions with Thyme

Beef Tenderloin with Foie Gras–Stuffed Morels

Pepper-Seared "Porter" Steak with Melted Leeks

Roasted Lamb Rib Eye with Sweet Garlic

Mushroom-Crusted Lamb Chops with Balsamic Jus

Braised Sweetbreads with Sherry Vinegar and Roasted Portobellos

Grilled "Giants" Cervena Venison Chops with Balsamic Glaze

Rabbit Saddle with Truffle Sauce, Snap Peas, and Pea Shoots

Sautéed Veal Medallions
with Thyme

Serves 6

This simple veal dish is perfect for entertaining, as the sauce can be made, the carrots readied for sautéing, and the leeks fried early in the day.

4 shallots
3 ½ tablespoons olive oil
½ teaspoon minced garlic
1 finger-sized bunch fresh thyme
2 cups fine-quality white wine
6 cups Veal Stock (page 189)
Coarse salt
Pepper
12 baby carrots
2 teaspoons unsalted butter
Twelve 3-ounce, ½-inch-thick veal medallions
2 tablespoons roughly chopped fresh parsley
1 recipe Crispy Leeks (page 193)

Peel and dice shallots. Heat 1½ tablespoons of olive oil in a large saucepan over medium heat. Add the shallots, garlic, and thyme and sauté for about 4 minutes, or until shallots have sweated their moisture. Add the wine and simmer, stirring occasionally, for about 1 hour, or until pan is almost dry. Add the stock and simmer, stirring and skimming occasionally, for about 50 minutes, or until liquid is reduced to 2 cups. Remove from heat and strain through a fine sieve into a small saucepan, discarding solids. Season to taste; set aside.

Peel carrots, leaving a bit of the green tops. Place in boiling salted water for about 3 minutes, or until just barely tender. Drain and refresh under cold running water. Pat dry. Melt butter in a small sauté pan over very low heat. Add the carrots. Season to taste with salt and pepper and sauté until just hot. Remove from heat and keep warm. Return sauce to low heat.

Heat remaining 2 tablespoons of oil in a large sauté pan over medium-high heat until hot but not smoking. Season 6 veal medallions with salt and pepper. Place them in the hot oil and sear for 2½ minutes. Turn and sear for 2½ more minutes, or until still pink and juicy in the center. Place on a warm platter and repeat with remaining medallions.

Place 2 medallions on each of 6 warm plates. Stir parsley into the carrots just to blend. Place 2 carrots at the side of each medallion. Spoon sauce over the top and garnish with leeks. Serve immediately.

A NOTE FROM JUDIE

If you season the meat long before placing it in the hot pan, the salt will draw out moisture and cause the cooked meat to be dry——not a good idea if you want a juicy, pink-in-the-center, very tender medallion. Charlie often serves these medallions on a caramelized Onion and New Potato Crêpe (pages 100–101). Although this involves much more work, the filled crêpes can be made ahead of time and reheated just before serving.

Beef Tenderloin with
Foie Gras–Stuffed Morels

Serves 6

Adish fit for a king! Tender filet mignon and rich foie gras held in the highest esteem by the earthy, smokey morel. Pure luxury at the table!

4 shallots
6 button mushrooms
1 tablespoon olive oil
3 cups good-quality red wine
1 Sachet (page 197)
8 peppercorns
8 cups Veal Stock (page 189)
Coarse salt
Pepper
1 tablespoon unsalted butter
18 large fresh morels (see Note)
1 cup uncooked Chicken Mousse (page 190)
½ cup chopped raw foie gras
1 tablespoon chopped fresh parsley
1 ½ cups Chicken Stock (page 189)
6 Potato Galettes (page 61)
2 tablespoons unflavored vegetable oil
Six 8-ounce, 1 ½-inch-thick filet mignons

Peel and thinly slice the shallots.

Wipe any debris from the mushrooms and roughly chop.

Heat the olive oil in a large saucepan over medium heat. Add shallots and mushrooms and sauté for 5 minutes, or until vegetables have sweated most of their moisture. Add wine, sachet, and peppercorns and simmer for 20 minutes, or until pan is almost dry. Add the stock and simmer, stirring and skimming occasionally, for about 50 minutes, or until liquid has reduced to 3 cups. Remove from heat and strain through a fine sieve into a small saucepan, discarding solids. Season to taste with salt and pepper. Cover and set aside.

Lightly butter an 8-inch nonstick sauté pan. Set aside.

Using a mushroom brush (or other soft brush), remove any dirt and debris from the morels. Evenly trim the stems off at the base. Carefully rinse and pat dry.

Place chicken mousse and foie gras in a food processor fitted with the metal blade and process until just combined. Scrape from processor bowl into a pastry bag fitted with a very small, round tip. Carefully pipe mousse into each morel, slightly overfilling. Place filled morels in prepared sauté pan. When all morels are in pan, sprinkle them with parsley and season to taste with salt and pepper. Add chicken stock and set aside.

Preheat oven to 200°F.

Place *galettes* on a nonstick baking sheet in preheated oven and allow to heat through.

Place a 12-inch sauté pan over medium-high heat. Add vegetable oil. Season filets with salt and pepper and place in hot pan. Sear, tilting pan occasionally to distribute fat evenly, for 6 minutes.

Return sauce to the heat.

Place morels over medium-low heat and bring to a bare simmer to just poach. Do not boil.

Carefully turn the filets and sear for an additional 5 minutes for rare. Remove from heat and allow to rest on a warm platter.

Place a *galette* in the center of each of 6 warm plates. Rest a filet, slightly askew, on top. Using a slotted spoon, carefully lift 3 morels out of their liquid and place them around a filet. Raise heat under morel liquid and rapidly boil for about 3 minutes, or until reduced to ¾ cup. Spoon equal portions of sauce over the filets. Pour remaining sauce in a gravy boat to be passed on the side. Drizzle some reduced morel juice around the edge of the plate and over the morels. Serve immediately.

SUGGESTED WINE: A first-class Bordeaux, such as Château Margaux, Château Latour, or Château Lafite

Pepper-Seared "Porter" Steak with Melted Leeks

Serves 6

A hearty red meat for a really hungry crowd. The rich, dark-brown flavor of the porter permeates the steak (and gives a double meaning to the word *sauce*). The strip steak is a porterhouse minus the bone and tenderloin. Make sure that the butcher cuts the steaks at least 1½ inches thick. If they are too thin, they will quickly overcook and be tasteless.

3 shallots
1 medium carrot
8 button mushrooms
3 tablespoons corn oil
8 peppercorns
1 tablespoon honey
2¼ cups porter, dark beer, or amber ale
8 cups Veal Stock (page 189)
Coarse salt
Pepper
1 bunch fresh Italian parsley
6 medium leeks
1½ cups Chicken Stock (page 189)
5 tablespoons unsalted butter
1 cup diced onion
2 tablespoons chopped fresh thyme
Six 10-ounce, 1½-inch-thick sirloin strip steaks, trimmed of all fat
6 tablespoons cracked black pepper

Peel and slice shallots and carrot. Wipe mushrooms clean of any debris and slice, lengthwise.

Heat 1 tablespoon of corn oil in a large saucepan over medium heat. Add the shallots, carrot, mushrooms, and peppercorns. Sauté for about 6 minutes, or until vegetables are lightly browned. Stir in the honey and sauté for 3 minutes, or until vegetables are caramelized. Add the porter and simmer until liquid is reduced by two-thirds. Add the veal stock and simmer, stirring and skimming occasionally, for about 1 hour, or until liquid is reduced to 2½ cups. Remove from heat and strain through a fine sieve into a small saucepan, discarding solids. Season to taste with salt and pepper. Cover and set aside.

Wash and dry the parsley. Set aside.

Trim off the green parts from the leeks. Split them in half, lengthwise, down to but not through the root ends. Holding the leeks together, rinse thoroughly under cold running water to remove all grit. Pat dry. Place in a medium saucepan and add chicken stock. 2 tablespoons of butter. parsley. and salt and pepper to taste. Bring to a simmer over medium heat. Cover and simmer for 15 minutes. or until leeks are meltingly soft. Remove from heat and keep warm.

Heat a medium sauté pan over medium heat. Add remaining 2 tablespoons of corn oil. When hot. add onion and cook for about 10 minutes. or until translucent and slightly caramelized. Stir in thyme and salt and pepper to taste. Remove from heat and keep warm.

Return the sauce to low heat.

Line a baking sheet with paper towels. Set aside.

Place a large cast-iron skillet on a cold burner. Add remaining 3 tablespoons of butter and turn on the heat to low. When the butter has melted. raise heat to high.

Season steaks with salt and press cracked pepper into both sides. Place in the hot pan and sear for 6 to 8 minutes. or until a nice crust forms. Turn and sear for 4 minutes for medium-rare. Remove to prepared baking sheet and let rest for 2 minutes.

Raise heat under the sauce. Add reserved onion and bring to a boil.

Place a steak in the center of each of 6 warm plates. Spoon equal portions of onion sauce over the top. Criss-cross two leeks on top of each steak. allowing some of the leek broth to mingle with the onion sauce. Serve immediately.

SUGGESTED ALE: A dark amber ale. such as Samuel Adams

Roasted Lamb Rib Eye with Sweet Garlic

The Crisp Potato-Eggplant Tart adds great texture and visual appeal to the finished dish, but it is not absolutely necessary. However, since it can be made in advance and reheated, why not do it?

3 single racks of lamb
1 medium onion
1 large carrot
1 stalk celery
6 peppercorns
2 bay leaves
3 cups Veal Stock (page 189)
Coarse salt
Pepper
1 pound Swiss chard
2 tablespoons olive oil
1 ½ tablespoons chopped fresh rosemary
12 cloves garlic, peeled
1 Crisp Potato-Eggplant Tart (page 60)
6 sprigs fresh rosemary

Have butcher remove the eye from each rack of lamb, leaving a bit of the cap fat (the layer of fat that covers the eye) on the meat and chopping the bones. Reserve the bones and meat scraps.

Preheat the oven to 400°F.

Peel and trim onion and carrot. Wash and trim celery. Dice the onion and cut the carrot and celery, crosswise, into ½-inch-thick slices. Combine vegetables with the lamb bones and scraps, peppercorns, and bay leaves in a large roasting pan. Place in preheated oven and roast, stirring occasionally, for 30 minutes, or until golden-brown. Remove from oven and place over medium-high heat. Add 6 cups of water and the veal stock and bring to a boil. Lower heat and simmer for 45 minutes. Remove from heat. Strain liquid into a medium saucepan and discard the solids. Skim fat from the top of the liquid. Place over medium heat and simmer for about 30 minutes, or until reduced to 1½ cups. Taste and adjust seasoning with salt and pepper. Set aside.

Wash the chard and remove any tough stems. Place in boiling salted water to cover and blanch for 30 seconds. Drain and refresh under cold running water. Wrap in a clean kitchen towel and twist to squeeze out all moisture. Unwrap and set aside.

Preheat the oven to 400°F.

Heat the olive oil in a large ovenproof skillet over medium heat. Season the lamb with chopped rosemary and salt and pepper to taste. Place, fat-side down, in the hot pan and sear for about 3 minutes, or until nicely browned. Add garlic and sear the remaining sides until just browned, turning garlic as lamb sears. Place pan in preheated oven and roast for 10 minutes, or until medium-rare on an instant-read thermometer. Remove from oven and place lamb on a rack to rest for 5 minutes. Lightly cover and keep warm. Carefully pick garlic out of the pan, making sure no grease is attached, and add to the reserved sauce. Place over medium heat to heat through. Place potato-eggplant tart on a nonstick baking sheet in preheated oven to heat through.

Wipe lamb roasting pan clear of excess grease. Return to medium heat and add reserved chard. Sauté, adding 1 tablespoon olive oil, if necessary, for 3 minutes, or until heated through. Season to taste with salt and pepper.

Place equal portions of chard in the center of each of 6 warm plates. Remove tart from oven and, using a serrated knife, cut it into 6 equal pie-shaped wedges. Slice each rib eye into 6 pieces. Arrange 3 slices on top of each chard portion. Spoon some sauce, along with 2 garlic cloves per serving, over the lamb. Rest a tart wedge against the lamb and place a rosemary sprig in the center. Serve immediately.

SUGGESTED WINE: A Pommard, such as an '89 Domaine LeRoy

A NOTE FROM JUDIE

Color is the way to gauge great lamb. The paler pink meat will be very young and tender; as the animal ages, the flesh turns a deeper red and toughens. Lamb fat can be almost pervasive and strong-flavored, so make sure that you skim the sauce well.

Mushroom-Crusted Lamb Chops
with Balsamic Jus

Serves 6

I usually serve these chops on Sweet Onion-Risotto Cakes (page 79), which absorb the lamb flavor beautifully. A simple potato or rice dish, or even a pasta, such as orzo, could also work as a "catch basin."

6 large button mushrooms
1 large onion
1 ½ pounds lamb bones and scraps
1 Sachet (page 197)
1 ¼ cups red wine
6 cups Veal Stock (page 189)
¼ cup balsamic vinegar
Coarse salt
Pepper
24 fresh pearl onions
6 tablespoons corn oil
2 tablespoons sugar
1 teaspoon ground cumin
8 large shiitake mushrooms
½ cup dried shiitake or tree ear mushrooms (see A Note from Judie)
Twelve 4-ounce Frenched lamb chops (see A Note from Charlie)
3 tablespoons chopped fresh parsley

Wipe button mushrooms clean of any debris. Coarsely chop and set aside.

Peel, trim, and dice the onion.

Chop lamb bones and scraps into pieces no larger than 2 inches. Place in a large, heavy-bottomed saucepan over medium heat. Add the chopped mushrooms and onion, along with the sachet. Sauté for 1 minute. Stir in the wine and bring to a boil. Lower heat and simmer gently for 15 minutes, or until pan is almost dry. Add the stock. Raise heat and bring to a boil. Lower heat and simmer for about 90 minutes, or until liquid is reduced to 2 cups. Add balsamic vinegar and simmer for 2 minutes. Remove from heat and strain through a fine sieve into a medium saucepan, discarding solids. Season to taste with salt and pepper and set aside.

Peel pearl onions. Heat 2 tablespoons of oil in a medium sauté pan over medium heat. Add onions and sauté, shaking the pan often to lift onions up, for 5 minutes, or until onions are golden on all sides. Sift sugar and cumin over the onions, shaking pan as you sift. Add ½ cup of water and cook, shaking pan often, for about 5 minutes, or until onions are cooked through and well glazed. Season to taste with salt and pepper. Remove from heat and keep warm.

Trim stems from shiitakes and reserve for another use. Wipe caps clean of debris. Place in a food processor fitted with the metal blade. Add the dried mushrooms and process until finely minced. Scrape from processor bowl into a shallow container.

Season lamb chops with salt and pepper to taste. Press each side into the mushroom mince to form a crust around the meat.

Line a baking sheet with a kitchen towel. Set aside.

Heat 2 tablespoons of oil in a large sauté pan over medium-high heat. Carefully lay 6 chops in the pan and sear for 6 minutes, or until a crisp crust has formed. Carefully turn and sear for 6 more minutes, or until a crust has formed and the lamb has cooked to rare. Place on prepared baking sheet and lightly cover to keep warm while you cook the remaining chops as above, using oil as necessary.

While lamb is cooking, heat sauce over medium heat.

Crisscross 2 lamb chops in the center of each of 6 warm plates. Arrange 4 onions around the perimeter of the chops. Sprinkle equal portions of parsley over the top and drizzle sauce over the chops and around the edge of the plate. Serve immediately.

SUGGESTED WINE: A Barolo, such as an '86 LaRocche by Bruno Giacosa

A NOTE FROM JUDIE

Tree ears, also called wood ears, as well as many other types of dried mushrooms, are available in Asian markets. Do not make the chopped-mushroom mixture until just before using, as it will get too wet and not easily adhere to the chops.

Braised Sweetbreads with Sherry Vinegar and Roasted Portobellos

Serves 6

Since many people turn their noses up at sweetbreads without knowing exactly what they are turning them up at, I suggest trying this recipe as an introduction to this succulent meat. The presentation is deceiving enough that you can have your guests guessing what they are eating until the last bite is consumed!

2 ½ pounds calves' sweetbreads
3 tablespoons coarse salt plus more to taste
2 tablespoons white vinegar
4 cloves garlic, peeled
5 tablespoons olive oil
3 cups Mirepoix (page 197)
6 peppercorns
6 sprigs fresh thyme
2 bay leaves
1 ½ cups red wine
2 ½ cups Veal Stock (page 189)
18 Red Bliss, fingerling, or other small new potatoes
½ cup diced red onion
3 tablespoons melted, unsalted butter
Pepper
6 large Portobello mushrooms
½ cup sherry wine vinegar
3 tablespoons toasted mustard seeds (see A Note from Judie)
1 tablespoon chopped fresh parsley
6 sprigs fresh parsley

Place sweetbreads in ice water to cover. Add 1 tablespoon of salt. Lightly cover with plastic film and refrigerate for at least 2 hours or up to 12 hours.

Rinse soaked sweetbreads under cold running water for 5 minutes. Place in a deep saucepan with cold water to cover. Add vinegar, 2 cloves of garlic, and 2 tablespoons of salt. Place over high heat and bring to a boil. Reduce heat and simmer for 14 minutes. Remove from heat and drain well. Again, rinse under cold running water for 5 minutes.

Using a sharp knife, trim any veins, sinew, or fat from the sweetbread lobes. Divide into 6 equal portions, keeping the pieces as large as possible. Place cleaned sweetbreads on a plate that has been covered with a clean kitchen towel. Fold the towel up and over to enclose the meat. Invert another plate on top and lay a heavy weight (such as a small cast-iron skillet) on top. Refrigerate for 12 hours.

Preheat oven to 350°F.

Heat 2 tablespoons of olive oil in a medium braising pan over medium heat. Add the *mirepoix*, peppercorns, thyme, and bay leaves and sauté for about 7 minutes, or until slightly caramelized. Place the sweetbreads on top and pour the wine over all. Raise heat and bring to a boil. Lower heat and simmer for 2 minutes. Add the stock and return to a simmer. Cover, place in preheated oven, and roast for 40 minutes.

Wash potatoes. Place in salted water to cover over medium-high heat. Add onion and remaining 2 cloves of garlic and bring to a boil. Lower heat and simmer for 15 minutes, or until potatoes are tender when pierced with the tip of a knife. Drain well, discarding garlic cloves. Return to saucepan. Stir in melted butter and season to taste with salt and pepper. Cover and keep warm.

Preheat the broiler.

Brush the mushrooms clean. Remove the stems and reserve for another use. Place the caps, gill side up, on a small, nonstick baking sheet. Brush with the remaining 3 tablespoons of olive oil and season to taste with salt and pepper. Place under preheated broiler and broil for 2 minutes, or until mushrooms start to sizzle. Carefully turn and broil for an additional minute. Remove from the broiler and place in a 350°F oven with sweetbreads to roast for 7 minutes. (If you do not have a separate broiler, remove sweetbreads from the oven while you broil the mushrooms. Then continue with recipe.)

Remove sweetbreads and mushrooms from oven. Using a slotted spoon, lift sweetbreads onto a warm platter. Cover and keep warm. Strain liquid through a fine sieve into a small saucepan, discarding solids. Place saucepan over high heat and bring to a full boil. Add sherry vinegar and mustard seeds. Stir to blend. Taste and adjust seasoning with salt and pepper. Lower heat and simmer for 20 minutes or until reduced to 1½ cups. Remove from heat.

Place an equal portion of sweetbreads in the center of each of 6 warm plates. Place 3 potatoes and some diced onion at one side. One at a time, cut the Portobellos, on the bias, into 3 slices and place on top of each sweetbread portion. Stir the chopped parsley into sauce and generously spoon the sauce over the top. Garnish with a parsley sprig and serve immediately.

SUGGESTED WINE: An intensely fruity and complex wine with herbal overtones, such as Bonny Doon Cigare Volant

Grilled "Giants" Cervena Venison Chops with Balsamic Glaze

Serves 6

This is a tailgate tribute to my beloved football team. Win or lose on the field, they remain giants to this dyed-in-the-wool fan.

½ cup balsamic vinegar
¼ cup olive oil
3 tablespoons ketchup
2 tablespoons Worcestershire sauce
1 tablespoon coarsely ground black pepper
½ tablespoon salt plus more to taste
2 medium carrots
2 stalks celery
1 medium red onion
½ head Savoy cabbage
Six 8-ounce, 1 ½-inch-thick venison chops
2 tablespoons corn oil
Pepper
1 recipe Potato Galettes (optional; page 61)
½ cup Citrus Vinaigrette (page 193)
1 tablespoon celery seeds
2 tablespoons chopped fresh parsley
1 tablespoon minced fresh chives

A NOTE FROM JUDIE

Don't hesitate to use this marinade with steaks, lamb, or veal chops.

Combine vinegar, olive oil, ketchup, Worcestershire sauce, coarse pepper, and ½ tablespoon of salt in a nonreactive bowl. Whisk together until well blended. Set marinade aside.

Wash carrots and celery. Trim and peel. Cut into uniform 2 × ¼-inch strips. Measure out 1 cup of each. Place them in boiling salted water to cover and cook for 30 seconds, or until crisp-tender. Drain and rinse again under cold running water. Pat dry and set aside.

Peel and trim onion. Cut in half, lengthwise, and then into thin strips. Set aside.

Wash cabbage. Core and cut, lengthwise, into thin pieces. Set aside.

Prepare a charcoal fire or preheat a gas grill.

Trim chops of excess fat. Brush them with corn oil and season to taste with salt and pepper. Place them on a hot grill with bones away from direct flame. Cook for

30 seconds, or just until grill marks have seared into the meat. Turn and liberally brush some reserved marinade onto the seared side. Grill, turning and basting frequently, for 15 minutes, or until chops are medium-rare. Place them on a warm platter and baste with remaining marinade. If necessary, cover lightly and keep warm.

If you are using the potato *galettes*, preheat oven to 300°F. While venison is grilling, place the *galettes* on a nonstick baking sheet in preheated oven for 10 minutes to reheat.

While chops are grilling, heat vinaigrette in a large sauté pan over medium heat. Add the reserved vegetables and sauté for 5 minutes, or until cabbage is tender and vegetables are heated through. Toss in celery seeds, parsley, and chives and season to taste with salt and pepper.

Mound the hot vegetable slaw down the center of a warm platter. Crisscross the chops, bones facing up, over the slaw. If using, place *galettes*, slightly overlapping, on each side of the platter. Serve immediately.

SUGGESTED WINE: A Merlot, such as a '92 Matanzas Creek

Rabbit Saddle with
Truffle Sauce, Snap Peas,
and Pea Shoots

Serves 6

I usually serve the rabbit on a bed of Soft Polenta (page 86), which, I think, is the perfect foil for the Madeira-flavored sauce. It is easy to make in advance, so you might want to try it also.

Six ¾-pound rabbit saddles (see A Note from Charlie)
2 tablespoons corn oil
2 cups Mirepoix (page 197)
½ cup chopped button mushrooms
½ cup Madeira
6 peppercorns
4 ½ cups Chicken Stock (page 189)
Coarse salt
Pepper
½ pound sugar snap peas
1 cup fresh pea shoots (see A Note from Judie)
5 tablespoons unsalted butter
1 ½ tablespoons Truffle Vinaigrette (page 194)
2 tablespoons minced fresh parsley

Have butcher bone the rabbit saddles to remove the loins with flaps attached. Remove the tenderloins and place one on each flap. Roll and tie the flaps in place with butcher's twine. You should have twelve pieces. Reserve the bones.

Cut the saddle bones into 1-inch pieces. Combine them with corn oil in a large saucepan over medium heat. Cook, stirring occasionally, for 5 minutes, or until the bones begin to brown. Add the *mirepoix* and mushrooms and sauté for 20 minutes. Add the Madeira and peppercorns and stir to deglaze the pan. Simmer for 5 minutes, or until reduced to ¼ cup liquid. Add 4 cups of chicken stock. Raise heat and bring to a boil. Lower heat and simmer for about 90 minutes, or until reduced to 1½ cups of liquid. Remove from heat and strain through a fine sieve into a small bowl, discarding solids. Season to taste with salt and pepper. Set aside.

Wash and trim the snap peas and set them aside.

Wash the pea shoots and set them aside.

Preheat oven to 375°F.

Heat 2 tablespoons of butter in a very large, ovenproof sauté pan over medium heat. Season the loins with salt and pepper to taste and carefully place them in the

(continued)

pan. Sear, turning frequently, for 10 minutes, or until well browned on all sides. Place in preheated oven and roast for 5 minutes. Remove from oven and place on a warm platter. Cover lightly and keep warm.

Return pan to medium heat. Add the reserved sauce and cook, stirring constantly, for 3 minutes. Stir in 1 tablespoon of butter, truffle vinaigrette, and parsley. Taste and adjust seasoning with salt and pepper. Turn off heat but keep pan on burner to keep sauce warm.

Heat remaining ½ cup of chicken stock and 3 tablespoons of butter in a medium sauté pan over medium heat. Add the snap peas and sauté for 2 minutes. Add the pea shoots and sauté for 1 minute. Season to taste with salt and pepper and remove from heat.

Remove the ties from the loins. Place 2 on each of 6 warm plates. Spoon sauce over the rabbit and arrange equal portions of the pea mixture around the rabbit. Serve immediately.

SUGGESTED WINE: A light Pinot Noir, such as Oak Knoll from Oregon

VI. CHARLIE'S FAVORITE SEAFOOD

The key to sublime seafood is not in the hand of the cook but in the lure of the fisherman. For it is how a fish is caught, handled, and filleted that ensures perfection. The fact that I absolutely love both catching and eating fish has only heightened my awareness of the necessity of high-quality fish for culinary excellence.

Before the advent of modern fishing techniques, cooking seafood was very simple. You ate only what you could catch from what were pure, clean waters. Freshness and high quality were givens. It is now somewhat more difficult to have that assurance when purchasing fish from an ice-packed tray in a fish market or a supermarket seafood section. Nowadays, a fish that is "fresh" is not necessarily better than one that has been properly frozen. Fresh only means that the fish has never been frozen; it does not tell you how it was handled or how long it has been out of the water. Surprisingly, even much of the fish prepared as sushi comes from fish handled and frozen using the ultimate modern techniques.

For the home cook, it is, therefore, vitally important to make a connection to a high-quality fish supplier. This can be through either a fine-quality and busy fish market or an equally busy supermarket seafood counter. Brisk business ensures quick turnover! Look for a fresh, nonfishy odor, antiseptic cleanliness, attractive and functional displays, knowledgeable staff skilled at knifework, whole fish well packed in ice, cleanly cut fillets kept ice-cold over, but not in, ice, and good rapport between staff and customer.

Once you've chosen your source, learn how to spot perfect seafood. Great fish are solid yet resilient when poked. They have *no* odor but do have a light, very fresh, clean smell. The scales, if they have them, should be intact, with an almost aspiclike coating. The

eyes should be bright and unblemished. The gills should be a vivid red or at the least, bright pink. If you have any question, smell the gill area and stomach cavity, as these will be where deterioration will begin. If you detect any odor, say "No thanks!"

If the fish has been cut into fillets or steaks, they should be neatly and cleanly cut into the appropriate thickness for cooking. A good, clean cut will highlight the texture and distinctive flake of the fish.

Once you purchase great seafood, make sure that it is properly packed for travel: whole fish packed in ice, fillets layered flat and separated by paper, cooked shellfish packed in sealed plastic containers in ice, and so forth. Get it into home storage as quickly as possible and store it just as you saw it in the market. Top-quality seafood should be eaten as quickly as possible; if a day goes by, however, proper storage should keep really fresh fish fresh.

Now that you've established a friendship with a fishmonger and can recognize great seafood, it is time to take your knowledge to the stove—where, again, there are some rules. When cooking seafood, the greatest care must be taken *not* to overcook it. Don't be afraid to pierce a hole into the center to test for doneness—the hole will rapidly reseal. Fish, when cooked through to the center, will spring back to your touch. You want to remove it from the heat source while it remains translucent in the very center, however, as it will continue to cook in its own heat as it rests. Although my recipes list exact cooking times, there are so many variables, ranging from the thickness of fish to the temperature of the heat source, that I suggest you make it a point to familiarize yourself with the touch and texture of the raw fish compared with that of cooked. This will help determine cooking time as well as ensure perfectly cooked seafood.

Pepper-Seared Salmon with Three Mustards, Haricots Verts, and Red Onion

Salmon Steamed in Napa Cabbage with Roasted Shallots and Warm Citrus Vinaigrette

Roasted Cod with Parma Ham and Fresh Sage

Sautéed Grouper with Caviar Cream

Roasted Halibut "T-Bone" with Beef Juices

Red Snapper Sautéed with Carrot-Curry Broth and Vegetable Couscous

Herb-Braised Black Sea Bass with Garlic Spinach

Niçoise-Style Striped Bass

Seared Tuna Steak with Ginger-Sesame Glaze

Crisped Tuna Spring Roll with Wasabi-Onion Puree

Roasted Lobster with Truffle Butter and Basil-Essenced Potatoes

Sautéed Soft-Shell Crab with Citrus Brown Butter

Pepper-Seared Salmon with Three Mustards, Haricots Verts, and Red Onion

Serves 6

This is a long way from the old standard salmon with hollandaise sauce. I think that it is much tastier, and I know that it is lighter and better for you. This dish provides a wonderful blend of color and texture on the plate (see photograph on page 132).

2 medium red onions
½ pound fresh haricots verts *or tiny green beans*
2 shallots
3 tablespoons olive oil
2 cups Fish Stock (page 189)
1 cup dry white wine
1 Sachet (page 197)
¼ cup Dijon mustard
2 tablespoons mustard oil (see A Note from Judie)
Six 5- to 6-ounce center cut, skinless, boneless salmon fillets
2 tablespoons coarse salt, plus more to taste
4 tablespoons cracked black pepper
2 tablespoons all-purpose flour
2 tablespoons unflavored vegetable oil
1 teaspoon ground cumin
Pepper
2 tablespoons unsalted butter
2 tablespoons toasted mustard seeds (see Note, page 125)
2 tablespoons coarsely chopped fresh Italian parsley
6 fresh parsley sprigs

Peel and trim onions. Cut in half, lengthwise, and then crosswise into very thin slices. Set aside.

Trim beans. Place in boiling water for about 30 seconds, or until they are crisp-tender and the color has set. Drain and immediately immerse in ice water. Drain and pat dry. Set aside.

Peel and mince shallots. Heat 1 tablespoon of olive oil in a medium saucepan over medium heat. Add the shallots and allow them to sweat their moisture for 3 minutes. Stir in the stock, wine, and sachet and bring to a boil. Lower heat and simmer for 20 minutes, or until liquid has reduced to 1 cup. Remove and discard sachet. Whisk in the mustard and mustard oil, a bit at a time, until well incorporated. Pour into the top half of a double boiler over hot water and keep warm until ready to use.

Preheat oven to 150°F.

Line a baking sheet with parchment paper and set aside.

Season the salmon fillets on both sides with 2 tablespoons of salt and the cracked pepper. Lightly dust the belly side (or top) of each fillet with flour. Heat vegetable oil in a large, nonstick sauté pan over high heat. Add the fillets, belly-side down, and cook for 4 minutes, occasionally tilting the pan to distribute the fat evenly. Using a large fish spatula, gently turn the fish, taking care that it does not break apart. Cook for an additional 2 minutes for rare or 4 minutes for medium. Carefully transfer the fillets to the prepared baking sheet. Place in preheated oven with an open door to keep warm.

Using a paper towel, carefully and quickly wipe sauté pan clean. Return pan to medium heat and add the remaining 2 tablespoons of olive oil. When hot, add the reserved onions and sauté for 2 minutes. Add the reserved beans, cumin, and salt and pepper to taste. Toss to combine and cook for about 1 minute, or until heated through. Remove from heat and cover with parchment to keep warm.

Remove top half of double boiler to direct medium-high heat. Bring to a boil. Lower heat and whisk in butter and mustard seeds until blended. Taste and adjust seasoning with salt and pepper. Stir in chopped parsley.

Place equal portions of the red-onion mixture in the center of each of 6 warm dinner plates. Place a salmon fillet on top, spreading onion out slightly. Spoon sauce over the fish and drizzle around the edge of each plate. Garnish top with a parsley sprig and serve immediately.

SUGGESTED WINE: A Chardonnay with good acid, such as Iron Horse

Roasted Cod with Parma Ham and Fresh Sage

Serves 6

T̲he salty ham and pungent lemon-sage reduction offer a wonderful contrast to the mild flavor of the cod. The sweet cabbage provides a perfect balance.

Six 4- to 5-ounce cod fillets
6 fresh sage leaves
6 paper-thin slices Parma ham or prosciutto
½ head Savoy cabbage
1 medium onion
3 tablespoons unflavored vegetable oil
1 tablespoon ground coriander
Coarse salt
Pepper
2 tablespoons chopped fresh parsley
3 tablespoons all-purpose flour
1 ½ tablespoons cracked black pepper
1 cup dry white wine
½ cup blanched, finely diced carrot
Grated zest of 1 lemon
Juice of 1 lemon
1 cup Chicken Stock (page 189)
3 tablespoons unsalted butter
1 tablespoon minced fresh sage

Using a very sharp knife, slice each salmon roll on the bias across the center. Set the halves against each other in the center of each of 6 warm dinner plates. Drizzle vinaigrette over the top and around the edges of the plate. Lay a shallot against each roll and serve immediately.

SUGGESTED WINE: A Riesling, such as Herrenweg Turckheim Zind-Humbrecht

Roasted Cod with
Parma Ham and Fresh Sage

Serves 6

The salty ham and pungent lemon-sage reduction offer a wonderful contrast to the mild flavor of the cod. The sweet cabbage provides a perfect balance.

Six 4- to 5-ounce cod fillets
6 fresh sage leaves
6 paper-thin slices Parma ham or prosciutto
½ head Savoy cabbage
1 medium onion
3 tablespoons unflavored vegetable oil
1 tablespoon ground coriander
Coarse salt
Pepper
2 tablespoons chopped fresh parsley
3 tablespoons all-purpose flour
1 ½ tablespoons cracked black pepper
1 cup dry white wine
½ cup blanched, finely diced carrot
Grated zest of 1 lemon
Juice of 1 lemon
1 cup Chicken Stock (page 189)
3 tablespoons unsalted butter
1 tablespoon minced fresh sage

A NOTE FROM CHARLIE

Cod is one of my favorite fish. It is available year-round and is very lean and firm. The mild-flavored white fish balances well with many different preparations. You can always replace cod with haddock, hake, or pollock.

A NOTE FROM JUDIE

To me, this is a particularly appealing dish for the home cook. Much of the preparation can be done in advance, and the final cooking is simple and relatively quick. The finished plate is exciting and the tastes are a bit intriguing. A perfect dinner-party showpiece.

Preheat oven to 150°F.

Line a baking sheet with parchment paper and set aside.

Season the salmon fillets on both sides with 2 tablespoons of salt and the cracked pepper. Lightly dust the belly side (or top) of each fillet with flour. Heat vegetable oil in a large, nonstick sauté pan over high heat. Add the fillets, belly-side down, and cook for 4 minutes, occasionally tilting the pan to distribute the fat evenly. Using a large fish spatula, gently turn the fish, taking care that it does not break apart. Cook for an additional 2 minutes for rare or 4 minutes for medium. Carefully transfer the fillets to the prepared baking sheet. Place in preheated oven with an open door to keep warm.

Using a paper towel, carefully and quickly wipe sauté pan clean. Return pan to medium heat and add the remaining 2 tablespoons of olive oil. When hot, add the reserved onions and sauté for 2 minutes. Add the reserved beans, cumin, and salt and pepper to taste. Toss to combine and cook for about 1 minute, or until heated through. Remove from heat and cover with parchment to keep warm.

Remove top half of double boiler to direct medium-high heat. Bring to a boil. Lower heat and whisk in butter and mustard seeds until blended. Taste and adjust seasoning with salt and pepper. Stir in chopped parsley.

Place equal portions of the red-onion mixture in the center of each of 6 warm dinner plates. Place a salmon fillet on top, spreading onion out slightly. Spoon sauce over the fish and drizzle around the edge of each plate. Garnish top with a parsley sprig and serve immediately.

SUGGESTED WINE: A Chardonnay with good acid, such as Iron Horse

Salmon Steamed in Napa Cabbage with Roasted Shallots and Warm Citrus Vinaigrette

Serves 6

The colors, flavors, and ease of preparation make this a particularly appealing dinner-party main course. I usually serve the salmon rolls in the center of a bed of Israeli Couscous (page 84), but they also work well on their own.

12 shallots
2 tablespoons olive oil
6 large Napa cabbage leaves
1 ½ cups Salmon Mousse (page 191)
Freshly ground white pepper
Coarse salt
Six 2 × 4-inch, 5-ounce salmon fillets
1 cup Citrus Vinaigrette (page 193)
¼ cup Brunoise (page 197)

Preheat oven to 325°F.

Wipe shallots clean and free of loose skin. Place them on a small baking sheet and toss with olive oil. Place in preheated oven and roast for 20 minutes, or until tender. Remove from oven. Cover lightly and keep warm.

Place cabbage leaves in boiling water for 2 minutes, or until just blanched. Drain and immediately immerse in an ice-water bath to refresh, taking care not to tear or break the leaves. Lay out separately on paper towels. Cover with another towel and lightly press to absorb all liquid. Repeat if necessary to dry leaves completely. Trim off the thick stem portions so that the leaves will lie flat. Carefully trim down edges to make a large square the same length as the salmon. Lay leaves out, singly.

Using a spatula, carefully spread a thin layer of mousse over each leaf square. Grind a sprinkling of white pepper over the mousse. Then sprinkle on salt to taste. Lay a salmon fillet on the edge of each leaf and tightly roll up, as for a spring roll. Place in a steamer basket over boiling water (see A Note from Judie). Cover and steam for about 10 minutes, or until rolls are firm but salmon is rare in the center.

While salmon is steaming, place vinaigrette in a small saucepan over very low heat. When warm, remove from heat. Stir in *brunoise* and keep warm on the back of the stove.

Using kitchen shears, snip the skin from the shallots, taking care to keep them whole.

A NOTE FROM CHARLIE

These rolls should be a bit rustic, so don't worry if the edges are a bit ragged and the mousse leaks out as you roll. They should really look homemade.

A NOTE FROM JUDIE

If you don't have a steamer, you can make one by placing a wire rack in a Dutch oven or roaster. Add about ½ inch of water and place rolls on rack. Place over high heat and bring to a boil. Steam as directed in recipe.

Pat the cod dry. Place a sage leaf in the center of the top of each piece. Wrap a slice of ham around the fish, leaving sides uncovered, and stick a toothpick into the ham at the point where it meets to hold it in place. Cover and refrigerate until ready to cook.

Wash, dry, and core cabbage, keeping it in one piece. Lay the cabbage, cut side down, on a clean, flat work surface. Using a very sharp knife, slice the cabbage, lengthwise, into very fine shavings. Set aside.

Peel and finely dice onion. Heat 1 tablespoon of oil in a large sauté pan over medium heat. Add the onion and sauté for about 4 minutes, or until slightly brown. Add the cabbage and coriander and toss to coat. Lower heat and sauté for about 5 minutes, or until just softened. Season to taste with salt and pepper and stir in parsley. Remove from heat. Partially cover and keep warm.

Remove cod from refrigerator. Heat remaining 2 tablespoons of oil until hot but not smoking in a large, nonstick sauté pan over medium heat. Lightly dust wrapped fish with flour and cracked pepper. Lay the cod in the pan, top down. Sear for 3 minutes. Turn and sear on other side for 2 minutes, or until just rare in the center. Using a slotted spatula, remove to a warm platter. Place a piece of paper over the top to keep warm.

Add the wine, carrot, and lemon zest and juice to the same sauté pan over medium-high heat. Cook, stirring occasionally, for about 6 minutes, or until pan is almost dry. Add the stock and butter. Bring to a boil and cook, stirring constantly, for about 2 minutes, or until slightly thickened. Stir in minced sage and season to taste with salt and pepper. Remove from heat.

Place equal portions of cabbage in the center of each of 6 warm dinner plates. Set a piece of cod in the center of each, carefully removing the toothpick. Return sauce to high heat and quickly bring to a boil. Remove from heat and spoon equal portions over the top of each piece of cod. Serve immediately.

SUGGESTED WINE: A big, buttery Chardonnay, such as one from Long Vineyards

Sautéed Grouper with Caviar Cream

Serves 6

When cooking grouper, always make sure that the strongly flavored skin has been removed, or the taste will be tainted. A member of the sea bass family, the lean, firmly fleshed grouper is a meaty fish that can withstand much more interesting presentations than the standard side-of-the-plate lemon wedge.

6 scallions
2 shallots
2 tablespoons unsalted butter
1 cup Fish Stock (page 189)
½ cup crème fraîche
6 Potato Galettes (page 61)
3 tablespoons vegetable oil
Six 6-ounce skinless, boneless grouper fillets
½ cup superfine flour (such as Wondra)
Coarse salt
Pepper
1 tablespoon olive oil
¼ cup sevruga (or American sturgeon) caviar
3 tablespoons minced chives
12 fresh 4-inch long chive pieces, end points only

Trim scallions of roots and most of their green parts to make six 5-inch-long batons. Place them in boiling salted water for 2 minutes. Drain well and refresh under cold running water. Pat dry and set aside on paper towels.

Peel and mince shallots. Heat butter in a small saucepan over medium heat. Add the shallots and sauté for 3 minutes, or until transparent. Add the stock and cook, stirring occasionally, for about 10 minutes, or until reduced to ¼ cup. Whisk in crème fraîche and allow to just warm. Remove from heat and set aside.

Preheat oven to 300°F.

Place potato *galettes* on a baking sheet in preheated oven for 10 to 15 minutes, or until piping-hot.

While *galettes* are warming, heat vegetable oil in a large, nonstick sauté pan over medium-high heat until hot but not smoking. Lightly dust grouper with flour and season to taste with salt and pepper. Place, top side down, in the pan, tilting to distribute the oil evenly. Cook for about 7 to 9 minutes, or until golden. Turn and cook for 4 minutes, or until lightly brown and just rare in the center. Remove to a baking sheet. Lower oven temperature to 150°F and place baking sheet in oven to keep fish warm.

Quickly and carefully wipe sauté pan clean with paper towels. Add olive oil and return to medium heat. Add the reserved scallions and toss to just warm through. Remove from heat and reserve.

Return sauce to medium heat. When just warm, carefully fold in caviar and minced chives. Do not allow to simmer (see Note).

Remove *galettes* and grouper from oven. Place a *galette* in the center of each of six warm plates. Lay a grouper fillet on top of each. Generously spoon caviar sauce over the top, allowing it to run down onto the plate. Drape a scallion across the top of each plate and place 2 chive points into the grouper so that they stand straight up from the dish. Serve immediately.

SUGGESTED WINE: A fragrant, opulent white Burgundy, such as a Meursault-Les Perrieres Boyer-Deveze

Roasted Halibut "T-Bone" with Beef Juices

Serves 6

The halibut T-bone must be very thick—at least 4 inches—for this dish to work properly. That gives enough depth so that you can really "roast" the fish and still open the oven to baste it frequently. The more it is basted, the more the outside will caramelize, giving a honeyed contrast to the moist, snowy white meat near the bone. This roasted fish calls for a light red wine such as a Pinot Noir or even a Beaujolais, an exception to the traditional white-wine-with-fish rule.

> 3 large shallots
> 1 small white onion
> 1 medium carrot
> 2 tablespoons unsalted butter
> 2 teaspoons fennel seeds
> 8 cups shredded Savoy cabbage
> Coarse salt
> Freshly cracked black pepper
> Six 4-inch-thick skinless halibut steaks
> 1 clove garlic
> 2 tablespoons safflower oil
> 2 tablespoons extra-virgin olive oil
> 1 ½ cups strong Veal Stock (page 189)
> 1 tablespoon minced fresh thyme
> 12 fresh thyme sprigs
> 12 Herb-Potato Maximes (page 192)

Trim and peel shallots, onion, and carrot. Slice, crosswise, paper thin. Set shallots aside.

Melt butter in a large, heavy-bottomed saucepan over medium heat. Add the onion, carrot, and fennel seeds. Lower heat and stir to coat vegetables. Allow them to sweat for about 7 minutes, or until onion is transparent. Add the cabbage and stir to combine. Cook, stirring frequently, for about 30 minutes, or until cabbage is quite soft but not mushy. Add salt and pepper to taste. Remove from heat. Cover and keep warm.

Pat the halibut steaks very dry. Peel garlic and cut in half. Rub the halibut with the cut garlic. Season with salt and pepper. Set halibut aside. Reserve garlic halves.

Heat a nonstick, ovenproof sauté pan, large enough to hold the 6 steaks, over high heat. When hot, add the safflower oil. Carefully lay the very dry halibut steaks in the oil, flesh sides down. Sear for about 4 minutes, or until fish is golden. Carefully turn and sear on other side for 4 minutes, or until golden. Remove from pan and place on a dry platter. Reserve pan off heat. The fish will, at this point, be completely raw in the interior.

Preheat oven to 500°F.

Wipe any excess safflower oil from the sauté pan. Place olive oil in the pan and return to medium-high heat. When hot, lower heat to medium and add reserved shallots and the reserved garlic halves. Sauté for about 2 minutes, or until just softened. Add stock and thyme. Raise heat and bring to a boil. When liquid comes to a boil, carefully return the halibut to the pan. Generously spoon liquid over the fish. Place in the preheated oven and roast for about 14 minutes, basting every 2 minutes. When the flesh begins to pull back from the bone, remove from oven.

Place a mound of cabbage in the center of each of 6 warm dinner plates. Carefully set a halibut "T-bone" on top of each mound. Cover and keep warm.

Return sauté pan to high heat. Add ½ cup water and bring to a boil, stirring constantly. Taste and adjust seasoning with salt and pepper. Uncover plates. Strain equal portions of sauce over each halibut "T-bone."

Garnish each plate with 2 fresh thyme sprigs and place 2 potato *maximes* on each side of the steak. Serve immediately.

SUGGESTED WINE: A Pinot Noir, such as Iron Horse

Red Snapper Sautéed with Carrot-Curry Broth and Vegetable Couscous

Serves 6

Red snapper has a very sweet, delicate flesh that is low in fat. The combination of snapper and couscous makes this a particularly healthy dish.

1 medium yellow onion
1 stalk celery
2 cloves garlic
3 tablespoons olive oil
2 tablespoons curry powder
1 cup white wine
2 cups Fish Stock (page 189)
1 recipe Vegetable Couscous (page 85)
Six 6- to 7-ounce red snapper fillets, skin on
½ cup superfine flour (such as Wondra)
Coarse salt
Pepper
¼ cup vegetable oil
½ cup fresh carrot juice
2 tablespoons chopped fresh tarragon
2 tablespoons chopped fresh parsley

Peel and mince onion and celery. Peel and chop garlic. Heat 1 tablespoons of olive oil in a medium sauté pan over medium heat. Add vegetables and cook for 3 minutes, or until they have just sweated their moisture. Stir in curry powder and cook for 1 minute. Add the wine and simmer for 4 minutes. Stir in the stock and cook, skimming off any impurities that rise to the top, for 10 minutes, or until reduced to 2 cups. Remove from heat. Cover and keep warm on back of the stove.

Reheat vegetable couscous as directed in A Note from Judie on page 85.

Wipe snapper fillets dry. Using a sharp knife, score the skin in a crosshatch pattern. Lightly dust with flour and season to taste with salt and pepper. Heat vegetable oil in a 12-inch sauté pan over medium-high heat. When very hot but not smoking, add the fillets, skin-side down. Raise heat and cook, occasionally tilting pan to distribute fat evenly, for about 6 minutes, or until skin is crisp and brown. Carefully turn and cook for 3 minutes. Remove from heat and drain on paper towels.

Return sauce to high heat. Bring to a rolling boil. Add remaining 2 tablespoons of olive oil, carrot juice, and herbs. Taste and adjust seasoning with salt and pepper. Turn off heat.

Place equal portions of vegetable couscous in each of 6 warm, shallow soup (or pasta) plates. Carefully set a snapper fillet in the center of each one. Quickly spoon equal portions of broth over the top and serve immediately.

SUGGESTED WINE: A sumptuous, fragrant Condrieu from the Rhône Valley, such as one produced by Guigal

The stunning view of lower Manhattan from the River Café, where Charlie worked as executive chef for four years, was the inspiration for this snapper dish.

Herb-Braised Black Sea Bass
with Garlic Spinach

Serves 6

Black sea bass is lower on the true bass totem pole than striped bass, but I find it a fine-textured fish with sweet, moist flesh. A bit fatty, sea bass can be cooked deliciously by any method.

Six 6-ounce black sea bass fillets
3 tablespoons olive oil
3 tablespoons chopped fresh chervil
3 tablespoons chopped fresh chives
3 tablespoons chopped fresh tarragon
1 ½ cups Fish Stock (page 189)
Coarse salt
Pepper
1 recipe Garlic Spinach (page 63)
Juice of 1 lemon
1 recipe Salsify Chips (page 192)
12 fresh 4-inch chive pieces, end point only

Preheat broiler.

Trim fish to make neat fillets. If your fishmonger hasn't done so, remove scales (see A Note from Judie, page 144). Rinse and pat dry. Using a sharp knife, score the skin sides in a crosshatch pattern. Using 2 tablespoons of olive oil, generously coat each side.

Combine herbs and toss to blend. Evenly sprinkle herb mixture on both sides of the fillets. Lay them, in a single layer, in a nonreactive baking dish. Pour in enough stock to come halfway up the fillets. Season to taste with salt and pepper. Place under preheated broiler, approximately 6 inches from flame, and broil for 12 minutes, or until fish begins to brown lightly.

While fish is broiling, prepare Garlic Spinach.

Remove fish from broiler. Place fillets on a warm platter and cover to keep warm. Pour liquid into a small saucepan over high heat. Bring to a boil and boil for about 5 minutes, or until reduced to ½ cup. Stir in the remaining tablespoon of olive oil and the lemon juice. Taste and adjust seasoning with salt and pepper.

Place a mound of spinach in the center of each of 6 warm dinner plates. Place a fillet on top of each and spoon sauce over the top. Place a stack of Salsify Chips on top. Gently push 2 chives into the salsify to form a V. Serve immediately.

Niçoise-Style Striped Bass

Serves 6

The inspiration for this dish comes from the much-acclaimed Chef Alain Ducasse of Monaco's Le Louis XV. His sea bass with preserved tomato and Niçoise garnish is one of my favorite memories of a French summer. It is absolutely the essence of the Mediterranean.

3 large, very ripe tomatoes
Six 6-ounce skinless, boneless striped bass fillets
½ cup extra-virgin olive oil
Coarse salt
Cracked black pepper
¼ cup chopped fresh parsley
1 ½ cups Fish Stock (page 189)
¾ cup tomato juice
2 tablespoons fresh lemon juice
¼ cup chopped, pitted Niçoise olives
12 cloves Roasted Garlic (page 197), skinned
2 tablespoons unsalted butter

Preheat broiler.

Peel, core, quarter, and seed tomatoes. Set aside.

Using a pastry brush, liberally coat a broiler pan and bass fillets with olive oil. Lay the fillets in the broiler pan, skin-side down, and place two tomato quarters on top of each fillet. Season liberally with salt and pepper and sprinkle with 2 tablespoons parsley. Refrigerate for 30 minutes.

Combine stock, tomato juice, and lemon juice in a medium, nonreactive saucepan over medium heat. Bring to a boil. Lower heat and simmer for 10 minutes, occasionally skimming foam from the surface. Stir in olives and roasted garlic. Remove from heat and keep warm.

Place the fish under preheated broiler, about 5 inches from the flame, and broil for 15 minutes, or until fish is cooked through and tomatoes are lightly browned. If tomatoes begin to get too brown before fish is cooked, lower broiler flame and move pan further away from the heat source.

About 5 minutes before fish is ready, return sauce to low heat. When fish is ready, remove from broiler and place a fillet on each of 6 warm plates. Strain pan juices through a fine sieve into the sauce. Raise heat and bring to a boil. Stir in butter and remaining parsley. Taste and adjust seasoning with salt and pepper. Spoon equal portions of sauce over the top of each fillet and serve immediately.

SUGGESTED WINE: Phelps Vineyard Pinot Gris or one from King Estate, with a good balance of fruit and acidity

A NOTE FROM CHARLIE

I don't usually recommend a period of rest after seasoning, as the salt will draw out too much moisture. In this case, however, I want the tomato and fish juices to combine and bathe the fillets with flavor. Then, in the final mix, all of the pan juices blend into the sauce for concentrated savor.

A NOTE FROM JUDIE

To make this dish work, you must have 1-inch-thick fillets. If you can't find them, simply butterfly thinner fillets and fold the flesh over to make a thick piece.

Seared Tuna Steak with Ginger-Sesame Glaze

Serves 6

I serve this on Crisped Soba Noodle Cakes (page 78), which complement the Asian notes of the glaze. Any simple grain, however, would also be a delicious accompaniment.

1 medium carrot
½ medium onion
3 ounces fresh ginger
1 tablespoon olive oil
1 Sachet (page 197)
1 tablespoon fennel seeds
½ cup muscat wine (or sweet Gewürztraminer)
1 ½ cups Chicken Stock (page 189)
½ cup Veal Stock (page 189)
3 tablespoons unflavored vegetable oil
Six 6-ounce, 2-inch-thick tuna steaks
Coarse salt
Coarsely ground black pepper
2 tablespoons dark sesame oil
2 tablespoons unsalted butter

Peel and trim carrot and onion. Cut, crosswise, into very thin slices. Peel ginger and cut, crosswise, into paper-thin slices, separating out and reserving 10 slices. Heat olive oil in a medium saucepan over medium heat. Add carrot, onion, unreserved ginger, sachet, and fennel seeds and cook for 3 minutes, or until vegetables have begun to sweat their moisture. Stir in the wine and cook for 5 minutes, or until pan is almost dry. Add stocks and simmer for about 10 minutes, or until liquid has reduced to 1 cup. Strain through a fine sieve into a small, clean saucepan. Set aside.

Heat vegetable oil in a large sauté pan over high heat. Liberally season the tuna with salt and pepper and place in the pan, making certain that the sides are not touching one another. Sear for 3 minutes, or until a slight crust forms. Turn and sear the other side for 3 minutes for rare. For medium, sear for an additional 30 seconds per side. Remove from pan and allow to rest on a warm platter.

Bring the reduced sauce to a boil over high heat. Stir in the sesame oil and slowly whisk in butter. Lastly, stir in reserved ginger. Taste and adjust seasoning with salt and pepper.

Place a piece of tuna on each of 6 warm plates. Spoon equal portions of glaze over the top of each piece and allow it to run onto the plate. Serve immediately.

SUGGESTED WINE: A light red, such as a Petite Sirah

Crisped Tuna Spring Roll
with Wasabi-Onion Puree

Serves 6

The sweet onion holds onto the powerful wasabi, and together they create a wonderfully aromatic base for the rich tuna spring roll.

2 large carrots
2 large white onions
2 tablespoons sesame oil
½ cup white wine
2 tablespoons wasabi powder (see A Note from Judie)
3 tablespoons chopped fresh parsley
Coarse salt
24 large spinach leaves
3 large egg whites
2 pounds center-cut bluefin tuna
1 tablespoon ground fennel
Six 8 × 8-inch wheat-flour spring-roll wrappers (see A Note from Judie)
Approximately 4 cups safflower oil
3 tablespoons Chive Oil (page 196)

Peel carrots. Cut, lengthwise, into 6 strips, 4 inches long, 1 inch wide, and ¼ inch thick, reserving unused pieces for another purpose. Place in boiling salted water for about 45 seconds, or until crisp-tender. Immediately drain and refresh under cold running water. Pat dry and set aside.

Peel and dice onions. Combine with sesame oil in a medium saucepan over medium heat. Sauté for 3 minutes. Stir in wine. Cover and simmer for 8 minutes, or until onions have completely softened. Scrape into a food processor fitted with the metal blade. Add wasabi powder, parsley, and salt to taste and process until smooth. Scrape into a clean, medium saucepan and set aside.

Trim spinach leaves of all tough stems. Dip into boiling, salted water for a few seconds to just wilt. Carefully place in an ice-water bath to stop the cooking. Drain well and pat dry. Place the leaves in a single layer on paper towels. Cover with a layer of paper towels and gently press down to absorb any excess moisture. Let rest until ready to use.

Whisk egg whites until lightly beaten. Set aside.

Cut tuna into 6 logs, 4 inches long, 1½ inches wide, and 1½ inches thick. Pat dry. Using a pastry brush, lightly coat tuna logs with egg white. Season with fennel and pepper. Using 4 leaves per log, wrap tuna with spinach.

Lay out 6 spring-roll wrappers in a diamond position. Using a pastry brush, lightly coat the wrappers with egg white. Place a spinach-wrapped log across the

A NOTE FROM CHARLIE

Young bluefin tuna is usually lighter in color and more delicate in flavor than the larger (1,000-pound) fish, which is often deep red, with an intense tuna flavor.

Wasabi powder and spring-roll wrappers are available at Asian or specialty-food markets (see page 199). Charlie often serves this dish with a sauté of shiitake mushrooms and sugar snap peas. If you do also, just sauté them quickly and sprinkle the crisp vegetables around the perimeter of the plate.

You could make tiny hors d'oeuvre spring rolls in the same fashion and use the onion puree for an unusual dip. These would be a cocktail-party hit for sure!

lower point, keeping enough of the point uncovered to allow it to come up and over the tuna. Lay a carrot piece against the side of the tuna log. Fold lower-corner triangular flap over the log and press the point into it to seal. Fold left side into the center and then fold the right side in, keeping a neat shape. Roll into a tight cylinder. Repeat until you have 6 spring rolls.

Place onion puree over low heat.

Heat oil until it registers 350°F on a kitchen thermometer in a deep-sided saucepan or deep-fryer over high heat. Carefully lower spring rolls into the oil and fry for 6 minutes, or until they are crisp and golden-brown on all sides. Using a slotted spoon, remove them to paper towels to drain. Season to taste with salt.

Ladle a pool of onion puree in the center of each of 6 warm dinner plates. With a very sharp serrated knife, trim ends from the spring rolls. Cut them in half, on the bias. Place 2 halves against each other, flat ends down, points opposing, in the center of each plate. Drizzle chive oil in a freeform pattern over the onion puree. Serve immediately.

SUGGESTED WINE: A Mentage, such as a '94 Quenoc, Langtry Vineyard

Roasted Lobster with Truffle Butter and Basil-Essenced Potatoes

Serves 6

What better combination than the indulgences of lobster and truffle with the lowly potato to create symmetry for the palate? The unusual method of roasting ensures a bib-free meal.

Six 1½-pound fresh lobsters
3 tablespoons olive oil
2 tablespoons chopped fresh tarragon
2 tablespoons chopped fresh parsley
Pepper
2½ cups Chicken Stock (page 189)
¼ pound truffle butter (see A Note from Judie)
½ cup finely diced leek white
¼ cup finely diced carrot
Coarse salt
1 recipe Basil-Essenced Potatoes (page 62), very hot
6 fresh basil leaves

Bring about 16 cups of salted water to a boil in a deep lobster or pasta pot over high heat. Remove claws from lobsters and place them in the boiling water. Cook for exactly 2 minutes. Add tails and bodies and cook for an additional 1½ minutes. Drain well and place in an ice bath for 15 minutes, or until well chilled. Using heavy kitchen shears, carefully cut open shells and remove meat from bodies, tails, and claws, keeping claws whole and cutting the tails in half, lengthwise. Place meat on a platter and drizzle with olive oil, tarragon, parsley, and pepper to taste.

Preheat oven to 400°F.

Place stock in a medium saucepan over medium heat. Bring to a boil and cook for about 5 minutes, or until reduced by one-third. Stir in truffle butter, leeks, and carrot. Cook for 4 minutes. Remove from heat. Cover and keep warm.

Place a large roasting pan in preheated oven for about 3 minutes, or until very hot. Season lobster with salt and toss

to coat with the herbs. Place, piece by piece, in hot roasting pan. Roast in preheated oven for 7 to 8 minutes, or until just cooked. Remove to stovetop.

Place the hot potatoes in a canvas pastry bag fitted with a #8 round tip. Pipe equal amounts, slightly off center, on each of 6 warm dinner plates. Place equal portions of lobster, including a split tail and 2 claws, around and on top of the potatoes. Drain the lobster pan juices into the sauce and stir to combine. Taste and adjust seasoning with salt and pepper. Spoon over the lobster and onto the potatoes. Garnish with a basil leaf. Serve hot.

SUGGESTED WINE: A rich, well-balanced white Burgundy such as a Puligny-Montrachet, Domaine Etienne Sauzet

A NOTE FROM JUDIE

Remember to save the shells to make Shellfish Stock (page 190), which you can use in place of the chicken stock. However, the more gelatinous chicken stock will make a smoother sauce.

You can use any size lobster you want, but the 1½-pounders will be adequate for normal appetites.

Truffle butter can be purchased by mail order from Zabar's (see page 199) or many other specialty-food stores.

Sautéed Soft-Shell Crab with Citrus Brown Butter

Serves 6

In the East, spring is heralded by soft-shell crabs and asparagus. I've combined them with the zest of citrus to really say spring has sprung. Try to keep all of the components very hot so that the plate virtually sizzles when it is presented.

> 2 lemons
> 2 oranges
> 18 medium spears fresh asparagus
> Coarse salt
> Pepper
> 2 tablespoons olive oil
> 18 live soft-shell crabs
> 1 ½ cups all-purpose flour
> ½ cup safflower oil
> ¼ cup (½ stick) salted butter
> 2 tablespoons chopped fresh parsley
> ¼ cup plus 2 tablespoons fresh lemon juice

Grate zest from lemons and oranges, taking care that you do not include any white pith. Set aside.

Peel off pith and, using a sharp knife, carefully remove citrus segments from membranes. Set aside.

Trim asparagus of tough ends and make stalks of equal size. Using a peeler, carefully remove outer skins from lower stalks. Place in boiling salted water for about 3 minutes, or until crisp-tender. Drain and refresh under cold running water. Pat dry. Place on a small baking sheet with sides. Season to taste with salt and pepper and drizzle with olive oil. Set aside.

Preheat oven to 350°F.

Wash crabs. Pat them dry. Using kitchen shears, snip off a piece across the front face area to remove the eyes and a small section of the lower mouth. Fold back each side plate on the underside and, using your fingers, remove the lung sacs. Place crabs on clean kitchen towels to dry slightly.

Line a sheet pan with paper towels. Set aside.

Combine flour and salt and pepper to taste in a shallow container. Dredge the crabs with the seasoned flour and set aside.

Place asparagus in preheated oven for 5 minutes.

Heat ¼ cup of safflower oil in each of two large sauté pans over medium-high

A NOTE FROM JUDIE

You can have your fishmonger clean the crabs. Even if you do so, wash and carefully pat them dry before cooking. The drier the crab, the less likely it will be to splatter when placed in the hot oil.

heat. Carefully lay crabs in the pans; be aware of the popping that occurs when any residual moisture hits the hot oil, as it can cause serious burns. Cook for 3 minutes, or until crisped. Turn and cook for an additional 2 minutes. Remove to prepared sheet pan and allow to drain.

Place butter in one of the sauté pans and return to high heat. When butter starts to foam, begin shaking the pan until it turns a walnut-brown color. Quickly, and in order, add zest, parsley, fruit segments, and juice. Immediately remove from the heat. Swirl the pan to blend the ingredients.

Fan 3 spears of asparagus, tips facing downward, on each of 6 warm plates. Arrange 3 crabs, slightly overlapping, on top of the asparagus fan. Spoon butter lightly over the crabs and serve immediately.

SUGGESTED WINE: A Sauvignon Blanc, such as Matanzas Creek

VII. DESSERTS THAT DAZZLE

No matter how spectacular the preceding courses may be, nothing elicits excitement at the table as does a masterful dessert. Memories of this last course are the ones that remain longest. It is where pyrotechnics are called for, where excess is allowed and encouraged, where calories are delighted in, and where more is truly better.

Dan Rundell, my pastry chef, his crew of sugar wizards, and I work together to try to invent plates filled with fantasy and visions of sugar plums. Our only requirement is that the flavors complement and balance one another. If the main component is chocolate, all of the embellishments must play with the rich chocolate flavor. If it is fruit, then the spices, sauces, and garnishes must respect the core element. Beyond this cardinal rule, there are no rules—just flights of fancy and sweet dreams coming together to say "indulge."

Many of our desserts have at least three to five components, but in most cases each component can stand alone. I hope that some of our ideas will inspire you to take dessert chances in your kitchen. So many elements can be made ahead of time that this is one course that makes it easily possible to overwhelm your guests with your creativity. Cut stencils in any shape you desire, usually no more than 10 inches at the longest part, from firm plastic lids or tubs to use for creating decorative *tuiles*. Purchase sheets of acetate from craft- or art-supply stores to make strips that will serve as linings for molds to ensure perfect frozen shapes. Keep chocolate cigarettes and spun-sugar sticks on hand for fanciful garnishes. Store sauces in plastic squeeze bottles with fine tips to use to decorate plates with fanciful squiggles. Make a supply of handmade truffles to serve with freshly brewed coffee. Advance preparation will make putting spectacular desserts together almost child's play.

Desserts that dazzle will indeed be the icing on the cook's cake. Served with one of my favorite dessert wines, such as Joseph Phelps Delice de Semillon, Swanson Late Harvest, or Bonny Doon Vin de Glaciere, you will find that they will make even a simple meal a memorable event. Take the time to incorporate them into your kitchen routine. Their payoff is its own reward.

Crunchy Flourless Chocolate Cake

Blueberry Financier

Warm Apple Pudding

Lemon Custard with Lemon Sorbet Lemons

Frozen Banana Soufflé with Walnut Nougat

Carrot Cake Soufflé

Chocolate Cointreau Truffles

Bailey's Irish Cream Truffles

Crunchy Flourless Chocolate Cake

Serves 6

This simple cake was originally made with the addition of fresh tarragon, which gave it a rather indefinable sweet-tart flavor that complemented the rich chocolate. If you choose to serve the cake without all the embellishments called for in this evolved recipe, you might want to return to my original by adding 1½ tablespoons of minced fresh tarragon with the final egg-white addition.

> ½ cup (1 stick) unsalted butter
> 4 ounces fine-quality bittersweet chocolate
> 4 large eggs, separated
> ½ plus ⅓ cup superfine sugar
> 1 recipe Chocolate-Bourbon Ice Cream (page 164)
> 1 recipe Deep Chocolate Sauce (page 165)
> 1 recipe Caramel Sauce (page 165)
> 1 recipe Chocolate Tuiles (optional; page 166)
> 1 recipe Chocolate Cigarettes (optional; page 167)
> 6 sprigs fresh mint
> 2 tablespoons confectioners' sugar

Preheat oven to 375°F.

Using 1 tablespoon butter, lightly grease six 2¾-inch or 3-inch round molds or a 9-inch round cake pan.

Place the chocolate and remaining butter in top half of a double boiler over simmering water. Heat, stirring constantly, until chocolate and butter are melted and mixture has blended.

Combine the egg yolks and ½ cup sugar in a mixing bowl set over hot water, stirring occasionally, until warm to the touch. Place in bowl of an electric mixer fitted with the wire whip and whip until doubled in volume. Using a spatula, fold in warm melted chocolate.

Place the egg whites in a bowl of a heavy-duty electric mixer fitted with the wire whip. Beat on the highest speed until soft peaks form. Add the remaining sugar and beat until egg whites are stiff. Using a spatula, slowly add one-third of the whites to the melted-chocolate mixture, mixing until just incorporated. Using a spatula, gently fold remaining egg whites into the chocolate mixture, folding together until completely blended. Pour into prepared pans and place in preheated oven. Bake for about 25 minutes, or until tops are springy to the touch and edges pull away from the molds (or pan). Remove from heat and place on a wire rack to cool slightly. While still warm, gently press down to flatten and then unmold into the center of each of 6 warm plates. Unmold the ice cream on top of the cake with the

A NOTE FROM JUDIE

It was Charlie's original recipe that showed me the level of creativity of a professional chef. I had made a flourless chocolate cake for years, but never once did I think to add such an unusual highlight——grated orange zest or a bit of liqueur, maybe——but never minced fresh herbs. By experimenting with recipes such as this one, it becomes easier for home cooks to stretch their culinary imaginations.

A NOTE FROM CHARLIE

I think the home cook will appreciate the fact that you can serve this cake simply garnished with a bit of confectioners' sugar and a sprig of mint or garnished lavishly with the sauces, chocolate *tuiles*, and chocolate cigarettes. An extra tip: I almost never garnish chocolate desserts with fresh berries as I think that the flavors clash.

rounded tops facing upward. Place sauces in plastic squeeze bottles (see page 160), and drizzle a stream of deep chocolate and then caramel sauce around the plate in an abstract pattern. If using, stick 2 *tuiles* in opposing directions, facing outward, in the center of the ice cream. Place an optional chocolate cigarette in the center and garnish with a sprig of mint. Lightly dust entire plate with confectioners' sugar and serve immediately. Alternately, cut large cake into wedges and serve dusted with confectioners' sugar and garnished with mint, whipped cream, crème fraîche, and fruit, or drizzled with dark chocolate sauce.

Chocolate-Bourbon Ice Cream

Makes 1 quart

Although a component of the cake presentation, this ice cream can easily stand alone. It also makes a new-fangled, old-fashioned soda-fountain sundae covered with caramel sauce, a dollop of whipped cream, and a maraschino cherry.

> *1 ounce fine-quality unsweetened chocolate*
> *2 cups sugar*
> *¼ teaspoon fresh lemon juice*
> *2 cups heavy cream*
> *2 cups half-and-half*
> *8 large egg yolks*
> *¼ cup Jack Daniels whiskey*

Using a sharp knife, coarsely chop the chocolate and set it aside.

Combine 1¼ cups of sugar with lemon juice in a medium, heavy-bottomed sauté pan over medium heat. Cook, stirring constantly with a wire whisk, for 10 minutes, or until the sugar has caramelized to a light brown color. Remove from heat and add chocolate. Gently stir until chocolate has melted and mixture is blended. Spread out onto a nonstick baking sheet and place in the freezer for 20 minutes to harden. When hard, remove from freezer and chop into very small pieces. Set aside.

Place heavy cream and half-and-half in a medium saucepan over medium heat. Bring to a boil and stir in ½ cup of sugar. Allow cream to just barely simmer, watching to make sure that it doesn't boil over. While cream is heating, place egg yolks in the bowl of a heavy-duty mixer fitted with the whisk. Add remaining ¼ cup sugar and beat on high speed until pale yellow and doubled in volume. Lower speed and slowly pour the hot cream mixture down the inside of the bowl while continuing to beat. When all the cream has been incorporated, scrape down the bowl with a rubber spatula. Add the whiskey and beat until well combined. Strain through a fine sieve into a clean bowl.

Place the bowl in an ice-water bath and, stirring frequently, allow to cool. When cool, pour into an electric ice-cream maker and freeze according to manufacturer's directions. When semifrozen, fold in reserved chocolate-caramel crunch and continue to freeze until just slightly firm.

Scrape the ice cream into a pastry bag fitted with a large, round tip and pipe it into six 2¾-inch domed molds. Carefully tamp down and level off the tops with a metal spatula. Seal each one with a sheet of plastic film and place in the freezer. Freeze for at least 2 hours, or until solid. When ready to serve, unmold by wrapping a warm, damp kitchen towel around the mold. Alternatively, serve directly from the ice-cream machine or scrape from ice-cream machine and store, airtight, in the freezer section of your refrigerator for up to 2 weeks.

Deep Chocolate Sauce

Makes about 1½ cups

8 ounces fine-quality bittersweet chocolate
½ cup heavy cream
1 ½ tablespoons unsalted butter

Using a sharp knife, chop the chocolate into small pieces. Set aside.

Place heavy cream and butter in a small saucepan over low heat and bring to a boil. Remove from heat and add the chopped chocolate. Stir constantly for about 4 minutes, or until chocolate has melted. Reheat over a hot-water bath if necessary to finish melting chocolate. If sauce is too thick, thin with hot water, ½ teaspoon at a time.

Serve warm or store, covered and refrigerated, for up to 2 weeks. Reheat to serve.

Caramel Sauce

Makes about 3 cups

1 ¾ cups sugar
1 ¾ cups heavy cream

Combine sugar and enough water to dissolve it (approximately ¼ to ⅓ cup) in a small saucepan, stirring until sugar has dissolved. Wash down the sides of the saucepan with a wet pastry brush to remove any sugar crystals. Place pan over high heat and bring to a boil. Lower heat and simmer for 10 minutes, or until liquid has turned light amber.

Place cream in a small saucepan over medium heat. Bring to just a boil, watching carefully to prevent spillover.

When sugar syrup is amber, slowly and carefully whisk in hot cream. When all cream is blended in, remove from heat. Place in an ice-water bath and, stirring frequently, allow to cool slightly. Serve warm or at room temperature. Alternately, store, covered and refrigerated, for up to 2 weeks. Reheat to serve.

Chocolate Tuiles

Tuiles are very thin, very crisp cookies made from a rather stiff batter. Baked in the traditional rectangular shape, the cookies are usually cooled over a rounded form to set into a gently curved shape resembling a classic French roof tile (*tuile*). We form the batter into a variety of shapes that are then used to heighten dessert presentations.

> 1 cup (2 sticks) unsalted butter, softened
> ½ cup mildly flavored honey
> 2 cups confectioners' sugar, sifted
> 1 ½ cups all-purpose flour, sifted
> ½ cup Valhrona light cocoa powder, sifted
> ½ cup egg whites
> 1 diamond-shaped stencil (see page 160), about 10 inches long and 2 inches
>   wide at the center

Preheat oven to 300°F.

Place butter and honey in a mixing bowl. Beat, using an electric mixer, until smooth and creamy.

Combine the sugar, flour, and cocoa. Gradually beat into the creamed mixture, mixing until well incorporated. At low speed, gradually add the egg whites. When incorporated, increase speed to high and beat for 5 minutes, or until a very smooth paste has formed.

Place a diamond-shaped stencil on a nonstick baking sheet (or cover a baking sheet with parchment paper and spray lightly with nonstick vegetable spray).

Using a spatula, spread a thin layer of *tuile* batter over the stencil. Lift the stencil up and repeat to make 14 diamond shapes (extras will allow for breakage). Place them in preheated oven and bake for about 10 minutes, or until the dough is slightly firm and not sticky to the touch and the edges are golden.

Remove from the oven (but leave the oven on) and either form the *tuiles* over a rounded mold (such as an inverted bowl or cup or a rolling pin) or mold them freeform into the desired shape. Work quickly, as the batter will set almost immediately. Reheat in the oven if necessary to make the *tuiles* pliable enough to form.

Cool on wire rack. Store in an airtight container for up to 1 week.

NOTE: To pierce *tuiles*, as soon as they are removed from the oven, using the point of a #10 pastry tip, poke a hole about ³⁄₁₆ inch in diameter in the center of the *tuile* about 1 inch from the end. Reheat as suggested if necessary to make the *tuiles* soft enough to pierce. This step is necessary when a recipe requires that sugar or chocolate sticks be inserted into the crisp *tuile* for the final presentation.

Chocolate Cigarettes

Makes 12 to 16

Chocolate cigarettes are simply large chocolate curls. They are not made from solid blocks of chocolate; rather, professional quality high-gloss coating chocolate called *couverture* is melted and allowed to just set and is then quickly and carefully scraped to form the curled shape.

4 ounces Valhrona dark chocolate couverture

Place *couverture* in the top half of a double boiler over boiling water, stirring frequently until melted.

Gently pour chocolate onto a clean, flat, cool work space or a flat baking sheet (*center right*). Spread the chocolate out about ¹⁄₁₆ inch thick and allow it to just set. A perfect sheen on the surface will let you know when this has occurred.

Using a stiff vegetable scraper held at a 45-degree angle, carefully scrape along an edge to test a chocolate curl (*bottom right*). If you wait too long, the chocolate will break off rather than curl. If it's too early, it will not shave off at all.

Square off two edges of the set chocolate. Place the blade of the vegetable scraper into the chocolate at the desired width and, in one motion, scrape up about 3 inches to make a continuous curl. Carefully remove the curled cigarette shape using the tines of a large cooking fork or a skewer. Do not handle or the chocolate will begin to melt. Continue curling the chocolate until you have the desired number of cigarettes. Finished cigarettes may be stored, layered between wax paper or parchment, in an airtight container in a cool spot for up to 1 month. Do not refrigerate.

NOTE: Chocolate couverture is available from many specialty food stores, candy supply stores, as well as from many of the sources listed on page 199.

Blueberry Financier

Serves 6

A *financier* is a classic French sponge cake, usually made with nut flour. Here we add blueberries, *sabayon*, and sorbet to raise a simple cake to new heights. It can easily stand on its own, however, dusted with confectioners' sugar and garnished with a few fresh blueberries and a sprig of mint.

1 cup (2 sticks) plus 2 tablespoons unsalted butter
1 cup fresh blueberries
3 ½ cups confectioners' sugar
½ cup plus 1 tablespoon all-purpose flour
½ cup plus 1 tablespoon blanched almond flour (see Note, page 170)
7 large egg whites
1 tablespoon freshly grated lemon zest
1 ounce fresh lemon verbena (see Note, page 170), chopped
1 recipe Blueberry Compote (page 170)
1 recipe Lemon Verbena Sabayon (page 171)
1 recipe Buttermilk Sorbet (page 171)
6 fresh mint sprigs

Preheat oven to 300°F.

Using 2 tablespoons of butter, lightly grease and then flour six 2¾-inch round molds. Set aside.

Wash and dry blueberries, making certain that they are clean of all stem pieces. Set aside.

Place remaining cup of butter in a small sauté pan over low heat. Allow to melt and cook for about 5 minutes, or until very aromatic and light brown. Remove from heat and keep warm.

Sift together 2½ cups of confectioners' sugar, all-purpose flour, and almond flour and place in bowl of an electric mixer fitted with the wire whip. Add the egg whites and mix, on low speed, until well blended. Scrape down bowl and slowly blend in warm brown butter. Raise speed and beat until well combined. Add lemon zest and verbena and beat until well combined. Remove bowl from mixer and, using a spatula, gently fold in reserved blueberries, taking care not to break them apart. When well blended, pour into prepared molds.

Place the molds in preheated oven and bake for about 20 minutes, or until tops are firm to the touch and golden-brown and a cake tester inserted in the center comes out clean. Remove from oven and place on wire rack to cool slightly.

While still warm, invert onto the wire rack. Place remaining cup confectioners' sugar in a fine sieve and lightly dust each *financier*. Place one in the center of each of six warm plates. Place equal portions of blueberry compote around the edge of

(continued)

each *financier*. Dot compote with *sabayon*. Place one scoop of sorbet on top of the *financier*. Again, dust the whole plate with confectioners' sugar. Garnish the sorbet with a mint sprig and serve immediately.

NOTE: Blanched almond flour and lemon verbena are available from many specialty food stores or from Dean & DeLuca or Balducci's (see sources, page 199).

Blueberry Compote

Makes approximately 5 cups

This compote can also be used as a topping for ice cream or plain cake.

5 cups fresh blueberries
½ to 1 cup sugar
2 sprigs fresh lemon verbena (see Note, above)

Wash and dry blueberries, making certain that they are clean of all stem pieces. Divide them in half and set one half aside. Combine remaining half with ½ cup of sugar, 1½ cups of water, and lemon verbena in a medium saucepan over medium-high heat. Bring to a boil. Taste and add additional sugar if necessary. Lower heat and simmer for 8 minutes, or until blueberries are soft and mushy. Remove from heat and remove and discard the verbena sprigs.

Pour mixture into a blender. Process for about 1 minute, or until a smooth, slightly thickened sauce has formed. Pour through a fine sieve into a clean medium saucepan.

Place saucepan over medium heat and bring to a boil. Remove from heat and stir in reserved fresh blueberries. Place in an ice bath and, stirring from time to time to ensure even cooling, allow to cool. Place in a nonreactive container. Cover and refrigerate until ready to use or for up to 1 week.

Lemon Verbena Sabayon

Makes about 2 cups

Sabayon is another French classic made by whisking together egg yolks, sugar, and an acidic liquid, often wine, over hot water to create a frothy, light-as-air dessert sauce. This sauce is perhaps best known as the Italian *zabaglione*, in which marsala combines with the eggs and sugar to make a rich partner for fresh berries.

> 2 large lemons
> 4 large egg yolks
> ½ cup sugar
> 2 teaspoons freshly grated lemon zest
> 2 teaspoons chopped fresh lemon verbena (see Note, page 170)
> ½ cup heavy cream
> ¼ cup crème fraîche

Juice the lemons. Combine lemon juice with egg yolks, sugar, zest, and lemon verbena in the top half of a double boiler over boiling water. Cook, whisking constantly, for about 5 minutes, or until thick and frothy. Scrape into a nonreactive bowl and cool to room temperature.

Combine heavy cream and crème fraîche and beat until slightly thickened. Gently fold into the cooled egg-yolk mixture, blending until well combined. Place in a fine strainer and push into a clean bowl to strain out all traces of zest and verbena.

Cover and let stand at room temperature until ready to serve.

A NOTE FROM JUDIE

Traditional *sabayon* must be made just before serving or it will separate. The addition of the creams makes our version much more stable.

Buttermilk Sorbet

Makes about 3 cups

2 cups buttermilk
¾ cup white corn syrup
¼ cup fresh lemon juice
3 teaspoons freshly grated lemon zest
2 sprigs fresh lemon verbena (see Note, page 170), chopped

Combine all of the ingredients in a medium saucepan over low heat. Cook for about 2 minutes, or until just barely warm. Do not overheat or buttermilk will separate. Remove from heat and strain through a fine sieve into a nonreactive bowl. Cover and refrigerate until cool. Place in an electric ice-cream maker and freeze according to manufacturer's directions.

Warm Apple Pudding

Who doesn't love apple pie à la mode? We just fancied it up to create this pudding. It's one of my favorite desserts.

2 ¾ cups sugar
1 ¼ teaspoons ground cinnamon
¼ teaspoon ground nutmeg
¼ teaspoon ground cloves
½ teaspoon vanilla flavoring (see Note)
8 Granny Smith apples
2 tablespoons unsalted butter
2 ½ cups cream cheese
¾ cup mascarpone cheese
¾ cup crème fraîche
7 large eggs
3 tablespoons fresh lemon juice
3 cups sifted all-purpose flour
3 ½ teaspoons baking powder
½ cup unflavored vegetable oil
½ cup milk
½ teaspoon pure vanilla extract
1 recipe Sour Cream Ice Cream (page 174)
1 recipe Cinnamon Tuiles (page 175)

Combine ¾ cup of sugar, cinnamon, nutmeg, cloves, and vanilla flavoring. Set aside.

Peel and core apples. Cut 4 apples into ¼-inch dice and cut the remaining 4 into thin wedges, placing them in separate bowls. Sprinkle half of the sugar-spice mixture on each.

Heat 1 tablespoon of butter in each of 2 large sauté pans over medium heat. Add diced apples to one and sliced to the other. Cook, stirring frequently, for about 5 minutes, or until tender. Remove from heat. Scrape into separate bowls and allow to cool to room temperature.

Beat cream cheese and 1¼ cups sugar until smooth. Add mascarpone and crème fraîche and beat until smooth, frequently scraping down the sides of the bowl.

Beat in 5 eggs, one at a time, frequently scraping down the sides of the bowl. Gradually add lemon juice, beating to combine.

Scrape into a nonreactive container. Cover and refrigerate until ready to use.

Sift the flour and baking powder together into the bowl of an electric mixer fitted with the paddle blade. Stir in remaining ¾ cup sugar.

(continued)

Whisk together 1 egg, vegetable oil, milk, and vanilla extract until thoroughly combined.

Add the liquid to the dry ingredients, mixing just to incorporate. Remove from bowl and shape into a flat disc. Wrap in plastic film and refrigerate for 1 hour.

Preheat oven to 300°F.

Divide chilled dough in half and, on a lightly floured board, roll out each half approximately ⅛ inch thick. Cut one half into pieces to fit either six 4-inch round by 2-inch deep molds or tart pans that have been lightly greased, or into an 8-inch round mold or tart or pie tin similarly greased. Fit the dough into mold or tin. Cut remaining half into appropriate shapes to fit the top of each filled mold. Remove chilled cheese filling from the refrigerator and pour it into dough-lined pan(s), filling no more than three-quarters full. Place equal portions of the diced apple on top of the filling in each pan.

Lightly beat remaining egg with 2 tablespoons of water. Using a pastry brush, lightly coat the edges of the lids. Gently place the lids, egg-washed-sides down, onto the filled molds. Press edges together to seal, trimming off any excess dough. Cut a small slit in the center of each lid. Place in preheated oven and bake for 45 minutes, or until golden-brown.

Just before pudding is ready, reheat sliced apples in a small sauté pan over low heat. Remove from heat. Cover and keep warm.

Unmold the individual puddings onto 6 warm plates or, alternately, cut large pudding into wedges and place on warm plates. Garnish each with equal portions of warm apples and a scoop of sour cream ice cream. Place a cinnamon *tuile* into the top of the pudding and serve immediately.

NOTE: Vanilla flavoring is available from Zabar's (page 199) or other specialty food or candy supply stores.

Sour Cream Ice Cream

Makes 1 ½ quarts

12 large egg yolks
4 cups heavy cream
1 ½ cups sugar
4 cups sour cream

Whisk egg yolks until well blended. Set aside.

Combine heavy cream and sugar in a heavy-bottomed saucepan over medium heat. Bring to a boil and remove from heat. Immediately whisk about ½ cup into the reserved eggs. Then slowly whisk eggs into the warm cream mixture. When well blended, whisk in sour cream until thoroughly combined. Strain through a fine sieve. Pour into container of an ice-cream maker and process according to manufacturer's directions.

Cinnamon Tuiles

Makes about 2 dozen tuiles

½ cup (1 stick) unsalted butter, at room temperature
6 tablespoons honey
1 cup all-purpose flour, sifted
1 cup confectioners' sugar
3 tablespoons ground cinnamon
3 large egg whites
1 stencil, no more than 9 inches long (see page 160)

Using an electric mixer, whip the butter and honey together until smooth.

Add the flour, sugar, and cinnamon to honey mixture, mixing until smooth. Slowly add egg whites, mixing until smooth and well incorporated.

Preheat oven to 300°F.

Place stencil on a nonstick baking sheet (or cover a baking sheet with parchment paper and spray lightly with nonstick vegetable spray, *top right*).

Using a spatula, spread a thin layer of *tuile* batter over the stencil (*center right*). Lift the stencil up and repeat to make at least 8 shapes (extras will allow for breakage). Place in preheated oven and bake for about 10 minutes, or until dough is slightly firm and not sticky to the touch and the edges are golden.

Remove from oven (but leave the oven on) and either form the *tuiles* over a rounded mold (such as an inverted bowl or cup or a rolling pin, *bottom right*) or model them freeform into desired shape. Work quickly, as *tuiles* will set almost immediately. Reheat in the oven if necessary to make the *tuiles* pliable enough to form.

Cool on a wire rack. Store in an airtight container for up to 1 week.

NOTE: This batter will make at least 24 *tuiles*. You can either bake and store them as directed or store the batter, airtight and refrigerated, for up to 1 week.

Lemon Custard
with Lemon Sorbet Lemons

Serves 6

Both the custard and the lemons can be served alone if you don't have the time to make the complete dessert. However, the components can all be made well in advance for a spectacular, last-minute presentation. You could also garnish the plate with a sauce such as the Lemon Verbena Sabayon (see page 170), substituting lemon zest for the verbena.

1 cup (2 sticks) unsalted butter
½ cup plus 1 tablespoon crème fraîche
5 large eggs
4 large egg yolks
1 ½ cups fresh lemon juice
1 ½ cups superfine sugar
1 tablespoon freshly grated lemon zest
1 recipe Clear Caramel (page 178)
1 recipe Lemon Sorbet Lemons (page 178)
1 recipe Candied Lemon Zest (page 179)
6 sprigs fresh mint

Generously grease six 3-inch round molds. Set aside.

Preheat the oven to 250°F.

Place the butter and crème fraîche in the top half of a double boiler over hot water. Heat, stirring frequently, until warm and well blended.

Combine eggs and yolks in a bowl over a hot-water bath. Heat, whisking constantly, until warm to the touch. Using a handheld electric mixer, slowly beat the butter mixture into the eggs. When well combined, beat in lemon juice. Strain through a fine sieve into the clean top half of a double boiler. Add the sugar and lemon zest and place over boiling water. Whisk for about 4 minutes, or until foam disappears from the top and mixture is warm to the touch.

Pour into prepared molds. Place in oven and bake for 30 minutes, or until custard is firm around the edges and almost set in the center. Remove from oven and refrigerate for 1 hour, or until set. Invert one custard onto each of 6 plates. Using a sharp knife, cut each one in half and turn so that the rounded sides are touching. Wipe plates clean. Pour some clear caramel around the edges. Slice frozen lemon sorbet lemon halves into wedges and set one wedge on top of each custard half. Garnish with candied lemon zest and a mint sprig. Serve immediately.

Clear Caramel

Makes ¾ cup

½ cup sugar
3 tablespoons warm water

Place sugar and ¼ cup of water in a small saucepan over high heat. Bring to a boil and lower heat to a simmer. Wash down the sides of the saucepan with a wet pastry brush to remove any sugar crystals. Cook for about 15 minutes, or until mixture has reached 320°F on a candy thermometer and becomes a golden-brown caramel syrup. Remove from heat and carefully stir in enough warm water to thin slightly. Immediately place in an ice-water bath to stop cooking and set syrup. Serve warm or at room temperature.

Lemon Sorbet Lemons

Makes 6

These delightfully refreshing lemons are easy to make and can serve as is for a quick dessert, with some homemade butter cookies for added interest.

1 cup sugar
3 blemish-free lemons
3 ½ cups fresh lemon juice

Place 2 cups of water and the sugar in a small saucepan over high heat. Bring to a boil and cook, stirring constantly, for 1 minute, or until sugar has completely dissolved. Remove from heat and allow to cool.

Wash the lemons and pat dry. Cut them in half, crosswise, and carefully remove all pulp and most of the pith, leaving very thin rind shells. Place in the freezer.

Combine lemon juice and 1½ cups of cooled sugar syrup. Pour into an electric ice-cream maker and freeze according to manufacturer's directions. When frozen, carefully fill each frozen lemon half with sorbet, pushing down on the tops to release all air spaces. Cover the tops with plastic film and return to freezer until ready to serve.

Candied Lemon Zest

Makes 1½ cups

3 lemons
2 ½ cups sugar

Wash and dry lemons. Using a citrus zester, carefully remove zest from lemons in strips at least ¹⁄₁₆ inch thick and 5 inches long. Place zest in a small saucepan with cold water to cover over high heat. Bring to a boil. Remove from heat and drain well. Repeat and drain. Again cover zest with cold water. Add 2 cups of sugar and place over high heat. Bring to a boil. Lower heat and simmer for about 20 minutes, or until liquid has become a slightly thickened syrup. Drain well, reserving syrup for other uses if desired. Place zest on a nonstick baking sheet, spreading it out to separate. Allow to set for at least 1 hour or up to 12 hours (until slightly dry).

Place remaining ½ cup of sugar in a mixing bowl. Add zest and toss to coat lightly. Return to baking sheet to set for about 12 hours, or until completely dry. Store at room temperature.

A NOTE FROM BOTH OF US

You can candy orange and grapefruit zest in this same manner.

Frozen Banana Soufflé with Walnut Nougat

Serves 8

Every component of this dessert can be made well in advance of serving. This done, each dessert will take only a couple of minutes to put together, so you can thrill your guests with little last-minute effort in the kitchen.

8 ounces Valhrona bittersweet chocolate couverture (see page 167)

6 tablespoons plus 1 teaspoon unsalted butter

3 cups sugar

1 cup coarsely chopped walnuts

2 medium-sized very ripe bananas, peeled

2 cups chilled mascarpone cheese

3 large egg whites, at room temperature

⅛ teaspoon fresh lemon juice

2 cups well-whipped cream

1 recipe Semisweet Chocolate Sauce (page 182)

8 Chocolate Tuiles, pierced (page 166)

8 Caramel Sugar Sticks (page 182)

Line a baking sheet with parchment paper. Place 8 circular metal ring molds measuring 2½ inches in diameter and 1½ inches high on the prepared pan. Cut 8 pieces of acetate (see page 160) into strips 2½ inches wide by 9 inches long. Set aside.

Place chocolate in the top half of a double boiler over boiling water. Allow to melt, stirring frequently. When melted, dip one side of the acetate strips into melted chocolate, one strip at a time. Place the chocolate-covered strips, uncoated sides against the mold, on the interior of the mold. It does not matter if ends overlap. When all molds are lined with chocolate, place them in a cool, dark spot to set. Do not refrigerate. *This can be done up to 10 days in advance.*

Use 1 teaspoon unsalted butter to lightly grease a baking sheet with sides. Set aside.

Place ½ cup of water and remaining butter in a heavy saucepan over medium-low heat. Cook, stirring constantly, for about 3 minutes, or until butter has melted. Do not boil. When butter has melted, gradually stir in 2 cups of sugar. Cook, stirring constantly, for about 10 minutes, or until sugar crystals have completely dissolved. Do not boil. Dip a clean pastry brush into warm water and brush down any crystallized sugar from the sides of the pan. When sugar has completely dissolved, raise heat to medium-high. Bring mixture to a boil. Gently boil, stirring frequently, for about 25 minutes, or until a candy thermometer dipped into the mixture registers 310°F (the hard-crack stage). Immediately remove from heat and quickly stir in the walnuts. When well combined, scrape syrup onto prepared baking sheet, spreading it as you go. Place on a wire rack and allow to cool. When very cool, chop the nougat into ½-inch chunks using a large, sharp knife. Measure out ¾ cup of nougat chunks and reserve. (The nougat may be made up to 2 weeks in advance. If so, cover and store in a cool, dry spot. Do not refrigerate.)

Place the bananas in the bowl of a food processor fitted with the metal blade. Process for about 1 minute, or until a smooth puree has formed. Scrape from the bowl and set aside.

Place the mascarpone in a large bowl and whisk until smooth. Set aside. Place egg whites in the large, grease-free bowl of an electric mixer fitted with a wire whisk. Place bowl into mixer so that it is ready to use.

Place a candy thermometer within easy reach of the stovetop.

Combine remaining sugar and ¾ cup of water along with the lemon juice in a heavy saucepan over medium-low heat. Cook, stirring constantly with a wooden spoon, for about 10 minutes, or until all sugar crystals have completely dissolved. Do not boil. Dip a clean pastry brush into warm water and brush down any crystallized sugar from the sides of the pan. When sugar has completely dissolved, raise heat to medium-high. Bring mixture to a boil. Gently boil for about 15 minutes, testing temperature frequently by dipping a candy thermometer into the mixture, cooking until thermometer registers 248°F (gumball stage). Do not stir during this cooking period. When the candy thermometer dipped into the sugar mixture registers 220°F, begin beating the egg whites at low speed. When they are frothy, increase speed to medium-high and continue to beat for about 4 minutes, or until stiff peaks form. When sugar syrup has cooked to 248°F, remove pan from heat. Pour syrup in a slow steady stream down along the inside of the bowl of egg whites, continuing to beat as you pour. Continue beating for about 8 minutes, or until a thick, shiny meringue has formed that is still lukewarm to the touch.

Use a large rubber spatula to fold the meringue into the mascarpone. When well blended, fold in banana puree and the chopped walnut nougat. Pack mixture into a pastry bag fitted with a #6 tip. Pipe equal portions of banana soufflé into the 8 prepared chocolate cylinders. Cover tops with circles of parchment paper and place in the freezer for about 1½ hours. You do not want to create a rock-hard soufflé. (This may be done up to 1 week in advance. If you do so, remove from freezer and temper in the refrigerator for 30 minutes before serving.) When well chilled, tap molds one at a time to release filled cylinders. This will happen quickly. Remove acetate strips and parchment tops. Place a filled cylinder in the center of each of 8 chilled dessert plates. Use a wet tablespoon to make smooth, quenelle-shaped mounds of whipped cream at the 10, 2, and 6 o'clock points on the plates. Place a piece of the reserved nougat on top of each whipped cream mound. Place the semi-sweet chocolate sauce in a squeeze bottle (see page 160) and make abstract squiggles of sauce in between each whipped-cream mound. Center a chocolate *tuile* on top of each cylinder. Place one caramel sugar stick in the hole. Serve immediately.

Semisweet Chocolate Sauce

Makes approximately 2 cups

1 cup semisweet chocolate chips
⅔ cup milk
2 tablespoons heavy cream
2 tablespoons unsalted butter
1 teaspoon pure vanilla extract

Place the chocolate chips in a small heatproof bowl. Place the milk, cream, and butter in a small saucepan over medium heat. Cook, stirring frequently, for about 4 minutes, or until butter has melted and mixture comes to a simmer. Immediately pour over the chocolate chips. Let stand for 30 to 60 seconds to melt chocolate. Whisk until smooth. When smooth, stir in vanilla. Set aside until ready to use. (May be made up to 2 weeks in advance of use, covered, and refrigerated. Warm in a warm-water bath before using.)

Caramel Sugar Sticks

Makes about 2 cups syrup

2 cups granulated sugar
1 drop fresh lemon juice

Cut about six 8 × 12-inch sheets of parchment paper and generously coat each side with nonstick vegetable spray. Lay sheets out on a clean, cool tabletop or marble slab.

Combine sugar with just enough water to dissolve it (approximately ½ cup) in a grease-free, heavy-bottomed saucepan over high heat. Bring to a rapid boil and add the drop of lemon juice. Brush down sides of the pan with a clean, damp pastry brush to remove any sugar crystals. Continue to boil for about 10 minutes, or until sugar syrup has turned a very light amber or has reached 310°F on a candy thermometer. Remove from heat and immediately immerse the pot in an ice-water bath to stop the cooking process (*bottom left*).

Working next to the prepared parchment sheets, dip the end of a wooden spoon (or a wooden dowel) into the hot syrup. Lift the spoon and stream the syrup, in thin lines, across the parchment (*bottom center*). Continue working until you have filled the sheets, leaving at least ½ inch between each line. When cool, chop off uneven ends with a paint scraper or metal spatula (*bottom right*). Lift the sticks and store them in an airtight container until ready to use.

A NOTE FROM CHARLIE

When you cook caramel syrup, I suggest that you use a copper saucepan, as it holds an even, steady heat and will not burn the sugar. If the syrup hardens, reheat it to soften. Caramel syrup can also be poured out into thin sheets and, when hardened, cracked into small bits to garnish desserts.

Carrot Cake Soufflé

Serves 6

This is a rather fancy version of the standard lunch-counter carrot cake with cream-cheese frosting. It makes a terrific dinner-party dessert, as all of the components can be made up to 2 days in advance of use. The soufflé can be put together and refrigerated early on the day of serving. The final baking should be done just before serving.

> 7 ½ tablespoons all-purpose flour
> ½ tablespoon ground cinnamon
> ½ teaspoon ground nutmeg
> ½ teaspoon ground cloves
> ½ teaspoon ground allspice
> ¼ teaspoon baking soda
> ⅛ teaspoon salt
> Pinch baking powder
> 1 large egg
> 2 tablespoons granulated sugar
> 1 ½ tablespoons light brown sugar
> 3 tablespoons vegetable oil
> 2 tablespoons honey
> ½ cup shredded fresh carrots
> 2 ½ tablespoons raisins
> 3 tablespoons chopped walnuts
> ¾ cup Clarified Butter (page 197)
> 4 sheets prepared filo dough (see Note)
> 1 recipe Soufflé Batter (recipe follows)
> ¼ cup confectioners' sugar
> 6 fresh mint sprigs

Sift together the flour, spices, baking soda, salt, and baking powder. Set aside.

Place the egg and sugars in the bowl of an electric mixer fitted with the whip. Whip for about 3 minutes, or until light and fluffy and doubled in volume. Slowly add vegetable oil and then honey and beat to incorporate.

Remove bowl from mixer and, by hand, beat in the dry ingredients, mixing until well combined. Stir in carrots, raisins, and walnuts until well blended.

Using a pastry brush, generously coat the inside of each of six 2¾-inch round soufflé dishes with clarified butter. Set aside.

Preheat oven to 400°F.

Line 6 luncheon plates with doilies and set aside.

Carefully lay one sheet of filo dough on a clean, flat surface. Using a pastry brush, generously coat it with clarified butter. Place three more sheets of dough on top, generously brushing each with clarified butter as you go. Cut the stacked dough into squares large enough to fit into the bottom of the soufflé dishes, and fit one square into each of the buttered dishes, ruffling the edges as you fit. Place about ¾ inch of carrot-cake batter into the bottom. Fill with enough soufflé batter to come up to ½ inch from the top. Using a small spatula, smooth the top of each soufflé. Place in the oven and bake for 20 minutes, or until tops have puffed and turned golden brown.

Remove from oven and set one soufflé in the center of each prepared plate. Place confectioners' sugar into a fine sieve and lightly dust the entire plate. Garnish with a mint sprig and serve immediately.

NOTE: Filo dough is available in the refrigerator or freezer section of many supermarkets and specialty-food stores.

Soufflé Batter

3 large egg yolks
⅓ cup plus 3½ tablespoons sugar
Freshly grated zest of 1 lemon
1 cup cream cheese
2 large egg whites

Combine egg yolks, ⅓ cup sugar, and lemon zest in a medium mixing bowl. Set aside.

Place the cream cheese and 3½ tablespoons of sugar in a small saucepan over low heat. Cook, stirring constantly, for about 4 minutes, or until cream cheese has melted. Remove from heat and beat about ¼ cup of melted cream-cheese mixture into the egg-yolk mixture. When combined, slowly stir remaining cream-cheese mixture into the eggs, stirring until mixture thickens. Cover and refrigerate for about 1 hour, or until well chilled.

Place egg whites in the bowl of an electric mixer fitted with a whip. Whip until soft peaks form, then slowly add remaining sugar and whip until stiff peaks form. Using a spatula, carefully fold egg whites into the pastry-cream mixture. Use as directed in the main recipe.

Chocolate Cointreau Truffles

Makes approximately 50 truffles

Truffles are the perfect ending to a fine meal. Easy to make, they are perfect to keep on hand for a divine dessert.

1 ¼ pounds fine-quality solid bittersweet chocolate
4 large egg yolks
¼ cup plus 1 tablespoon sugar
¾ cup heavy cream
½ cup (1 stick) unsalted butter
⅓ cup Cointreau
½ pound milk-chocolate couverture *(see page 167)*

Chop the bittersweet chocolate into very fine pieces and set aside.

Place the egg yolks and sugar in a medium bowl and whisk until well combined and pale yellow. Set aside.

Place the cream and butter in a small saucepan over low heat. Allow to come just to a simmer. Do not boil. Slowly whisk hot cream into the egg-yolk mixture, whisking until smooth. Strain through a fine sieve into a clean bowl. Add the reserved chocolate and beat until smooth. (If mixture cools down too much to melt the chocolate, place bowl over a hot-water bath as you beat.) Add Cointreau and beat to blend. Pour into a nonreactive container. Cover and freeze until you are ready to form the truffles.

When you're ready to make individual truffles, melt *couverture* in the top half of a double boiler over very hot water. Line a baking sheet with parchment paper. Remove truffle mixture from the freezer. Using a small melon baller, scoop out balls of truffle mixture and place them on lined baking sheet. When you have filled the sheet, return it to the freezer for about 5 minutes to chill. Remove from freezer and, using a dinner fork, drizzle melted chocolate *couverture* over the truffle balls to make milk-chocolate stripes. Place in refrigerator to set. When set, store in an airtight container and refrigerate for up to 1 week.

A NOTE FROM JUDIE

If you do not want the liqueur flavor, you can add about 1 teaspoon freshly grated orange zest to keep a hint of orange in the chocolate.

Dip melon baller in warm water and pat it dry before scooping to release the truffles easily.

VIII. KITCHEN BASICS

VIII. KITCHEN BASICS

Chocolate Cointreau Truffles

Makes approximately 50 truffles

Truffles are the perfect ending to a fine meal. Easy to make, they are perfect to keep on hand for a divine dessert.

1 ¼ pounds fine-quality solid bittersweet chocolate
4 large egg yolks
¼ cup plus 1 tablespoon sugar
¾ cup heavy cream
½ cup (1 stick) unsalted butter
⅓ cup Cointreau
½ pound milk-chocolate couverture (see page 167)

Chop the bittersweet chocolate into very fine pieces and set aside.

Place the egg yolks and sugar in a medium bowl and whisk until well combined and pale yellow. Set aside.

Place the cream and butter in a small saucepan over low heat. Allow to come just to a simmer. Do not boil. Slowly whisk hot cream into the egg-yolk mixture, whisking until smooth. Strain through a fine sieve into a clean bowl. Add the reserved chocolate and beat until smooth. (If mixture cools down too much to melt the chocolate, place bowl over a hot-water bath as you beat.) Add Cointreau and beat to blend. Pour into a nonreactive container. Cover and freeze until you are ready to form the truffles.

When you're ready to make individual truffles, melt *couverture* in the top half of a double boiler over very hot water. Line a baking sheet with parchment paper. Remove truffle mixture from the freezer. Using a small melon baller, scoop out balls of truffle mixture and place them on lined baking sheet. When you have filled the sheet, return it to the freezer for about 5 minutes to chill. Remove from freezer and, using a dinner fork, drizzle melted chocolate *couverture* over the truffle balls to make milk-chocolate stripes. Place in refrigerator to set. When set, store in an airtight container and refrigerate for up to 1 week.

Bailey's Irish Cream Truffles

8 ounces fine-quality solid milk chocolate
1 cup praline paste (see Note)
1 large egg yolk
¾ cup Bailey's Irish Cream
½ pound milk-chocolate couverture *(see page 167)*
¼ pound dark-chocolate couverture

Chop solid milk chocolate into small pieces. Place in the top half of a double boiler over hot water. Add the praline paste and warm, stirring constantly, until smooth. Remove from heat and allow to cool until still warm but not hot to the touch. Beat in the egg yolk. When incorporated, whisk in the liqueur. When well blended, pour into a nonreactive container. Cover and freeze until you are ready to form the truffles.

When you are ready to make the individual truffles, line a baking sheet with parchment paper. Melt milk-chocolate *couverture* in top half of a double boiler over hot water. Remove truffle mixture from the freezer. Using a small melon baller, scoop out balls of truffle mixture. Place on lined baking sheet. When you have made the number of truffles you desire, place entire sheet in freezer for about 5 minutes to chill.

Remove from freezer. Stick a bamboo skewer into each truffle and, one at a time, dip truffles into the melted milk-chocolate *couverture*. Gently push truffle off skewer with another skewer onto lined baking sheet. When all truffles are dipped, place in the refrigerator to set.

While *couverture* is setting, melt dark-chocolate *couverture* in top half of a double boiler over hot water.

Remove set truffles from refrigerator. Using a dinner fork, drizzle dark-chocolate strips over truffle balls. Place in refrigerator to set. When set, store in an airtight container in the refrigerator for up to 1 week.

NOTE: Praline paste is available from some gourmet and candy-making shops.

Chicken Stock

Makes about 8 cups

4 pounds chicken carcasses and/or necks and backs

1 tablespoon canola oil

3 medium carrots, peeled and chopped

2 cups chopped onion

2 cups chopped celery

1 ½ teaspoons dried thyme

8 peppercorns

1 bay leaf

Rinse chicken bones and pieces. Pat them dry and set aside.

Heat oil in a large stockpot over medium heat. Add vegetables and cook, stirring frequently, for about 5 minutes, or until just softened. Stir in chicken carcasses and/or pieces, thyme, peppercorns, and bay leaf. When well combined, add 1 gallon of water. Bring to a boil, then lower heat and simmer for about 3 hours, occasionally skimming off scum, or until liquid is reduced to 8 cups.

Strain through a fine sieve, pushing on solids to extract as much liquid as possible. Discard solids. Allow stock to cool slightly, spooning off fat as it rises to the surface. Cover and refrigerate for up to 2 to 3 days, or freeze in small quantities, for ease of use, for up to 3 months. Before using, spoon or scrape off any fat that has solidified on top.

A NOTE FROM JUDIE: If you want your stock to have a deeper, richer color and flavor, roast the chicken carcasses and pieces in a preheated 350°F oven for about 15 minutes before adding them to the stock. The rich stocks used in the restaurants are made by replacing the water in a stock with the previous day's stock. The intense flavor can't be beat, but it does take time and money to create this at home. Perhaps more than any other thing, the rich stock bases for sauces distinguish a fine restaurant meal from a home cook's dinner. If you consider yourself a serious cook, we recommend trying to make and keep on hand a batch of rich stock. You'll be amazed at the difference in the finished recipe.

Veal Stock

Makes about 6 cups

¼ cup plus 2 tablespoons canola oil

7 pounds veal knuckle and marrow bones

3 onions, peeled and chopped

2 carrots, peeled and chopped

1 cup chopped celery

1 cup canned tomato puree

1 ½ teaspoons dried thyme

8 peppercorns

1 bay leaf

Preheat oven to 350°F.

Using ¼ cup oil, lightly coat the bones. Place them in a roasting pan in preheated oven and roast, turning occasionally, for about 20 minutes, or until well browned. Using a slotted spoon, remove from pan and transfer to a large stockpot.

If necessary, add remaining oil to roasting pan. Stir in vegetables and place pan over medium heat on top of the stove. Cook, stirring frequently, for about 5 minutes, or until softened. Using a slotted spoon, transfer to the stockpot.

Pour fat from roasting pan. Add 2 cups of water and return to medium heat on top of the stove. Cook, stirring constantly, scraping any particles sticking to the bottom of the pan, for about 2 minutes, or until pan is deglazed. Pour into stockpot. Add remaining ingredients and 3½ quarts of water and stir to combine. Place over medium-high heat and bring to a boil. Lower heat and simmer for about 6 hours, occasionally skimming off foam and fat, or until liquid has reduced to about 6 cups. Strain through a very fine sieve, pushing on solids to extract as much liquid as possible. Discard solids. Allow stock to cool slightly, spooning off fat as it rises to the top. Cover and refrigerate for up to 2 to 3 days or freeze, in small quantities, for ease of use, for up to 3 months. Before using, spoon or scrape off any fat that has solidified on top.

A NOTE FROM JUDIE: Additional bones and meat scraps and further reduction will yield a richer stock. Charlie often uses what he calls "natural sauce" to garnish meat dishes. It is the deepest and richest of all stock reductions, created by combining a rich stock (see Note, above) that has been even further reduced with the addition of a reduction of red wine, shallots, and *mirepoix* (see page 197). Easy to do—just add some time in your kitchen and money to your grocery list! Use beef, lamb, or venison bones in place of the veal bones and follow this basic recipe for beef, lamb, or venison stock.

Fish Stock

Makes about 6 cups

3 pounds fish skeletons

2 tablespoons canola oil

2 medium onions, peeled and chopped

2 cups chopped celery

1 bulb fennel, washed and chopped

2 cups dry white wine

1 teaspoon dried thyme

6 peppercorns

1 bay leaf

Remove and discard heads from skeletons, if necessary. Clean the fish bones under cold running water to remove any trace of blood on the frames. Set aside.

Heat oil in a large saucepan over medium heat. Add vegetables. Lower heat and place a piece of waxed paper directly on the vegetables. Cook, stirring once or twice, for about 7 minutes, or until vegetables have sweated their liquid but are not brown. Remove and discard waxed paper. Stir in fish bones. Raise heat to medium and add wine. Bring to a boil, then lower heat and simmer for about 10 minutes, or until liquid is reduced by half. Add thyme, peppercorns, bay leaf, and 8 cups of water. Raise heat and bring to a boil. Lower heat and simmer for about 1½ hours, occasionally skimming off the scum.

Strain through a very fine sieve, discarding solids. Allow to cool slightly. Cover and refrigerate for up to 2 to 3 days or freeze, in small quantities, for ease of use, for 2 to 3 weeks. Before using, spoon or scrape off any fat that has solidified on the top.

A NOTE FROM JUDIE: Fish stock has a very delicate flavor that does not hold up well over long periods of freezing. Therefore, we don't recommend freezing it for more than 3 weeks.

Shellfish Stock

Makes about 6 cups

3 pounds lobster and/or shrimp shells and bodies
¼ cup plus 2 tablespoons canola oil
3 medium carrots, peeled and chopped
2 cups chopped celery
2 medium onions, peeled and chopped
1 bulb fennel, washed and chopped (optional)
1 head garlic, pulled apart and peeled
1 cup brandy
1 cup peeled and chopped ripe tomatoes (optional)
1 teaspoon dried thyme
6 peppercorns
1 bay leaf

Preheat oven to 400°F.

Place shells and/or bodies in a roasting pan. Drizzle ¼ cup of oil over them and toss to coat. Place pan in preheated oven and roast for 25 minutes. Remove from heat and, using a slotted spoon, place bodies and/or shells in a large stockpot.

Heat remaining 2 tablespoons of oil in a saucepan over medium heat. Add carrot, celery, onion, and, if using, fennel. Lower heat and allow vegetables to just sweat for about 5 minutes, or until almost translucent. Add garlic and cook, stirring frequently, for 10 minutes. Scrape into stockpot. Stir in brandy and place over medium-high heat. Bring to a boil. Lower heat and simmer for about 10 minutes, or until liquid has almost evaporated.

Stir in tomato, if using. Add 8 cups of water and bring to a boil. Skim off the scum and stir in thyme, peppercorns, and bay leaf. Lower heat and simmer for 1½ hours, occasionally skimming off the scum.

Strain through a very fine sieve, discarding solids. Allow to cool. Cover and refrigerate for up to 2 to 3 days or freeze, in small quantities for ease of use, for 2 to 3 weeks. Before using, spoon or scrape off any fat that has solidified on the top.

A NOTE FROM JUDIE: Like fish stock, shellfish stock has such a delicate flavor that it does not freeze well for a long period of time.

Vegetable Stock

Makes 4 cups

3 stalks celery
2 large carrots
2 large onions
2 large tomatoes
2 large bell peppers
2 tablespoons olive oil
8 cloves garlic, peeled
1 Sachet (page 197)
½ cup white wine

Wash, trim, and chop celery and carrots. Peel and chop onions. Combine them with carrots and celery. Wash, core, and chop tomatoes and add them to other vegetables. Wash, core, and seed peppers and add them to other vegetables.

Heat olive oil in a large saucepan over medium heat. Add vegetables, garlic, and sachet. Cook, stirring frequently, for 5 minutes, or until just softened. Add the wine and cook, stirring constantly, for 1 minute to deglaze pan. Raise heat, add 6 cups of water, and bring to a boil. Lower heat and simmer for 45 minutes, or until reduced to 4 cups. Strain through a fine sieve, pushing on solids to extract as much liquid as possible. Discard solids. Pour into a nonreactive container and store in an airtight container in the refrigerator for up to 2 days, or in the freezer for up to 3 months.

A NOTE FROM BOTH OF US: You can use almost any vegetable to make stock. Even vegetable trimmings can be added to the pot for extra flavor. However, the stronger-tasting vegetables, such as turnips or broccoli, will overpower the gentler flavors and make a very pungent stock. It is a good idea to freeze vegetable odds and ends so that you do not have to purchase stock ingredients.

Chicken Mousse

Makes about 2 cups

½ pound boneless, skinless chicken leg or thigh meat
1 large egg
1 egg yolk
½ cup heavy cream
1½ teaspoons coarse salt
1½ teaspoons freshly ground white pepper
½ teaspoon ground nutmeg

Cut chicken into bite-sized pieces. Place in bowl of a food processor fitted with the metal blade and process until finely minced. Add whole egg and yolk and continue processing to make a puree. With processor running, slowly add cream. When well incorporated, add seasonings and process to just blend. Scrape from processor bowl into a nonreactive container. Cover and refrigerate until ready to use.

Use the uncooked mousse as a filling for vegetable roulades or pastas that will be cooked. It may also be used to make quenelles that will be gently poached in a stock.

To use mousse as an appetizer or hors d'oeuvre, place in a well-buttered 2 quart mold lined with buttered parchment paper. Tightly seal with aluminum foil. Place in a hot water bath in a preheated 350°F. oven and bake for about 20 minutes, or until mousse is cooked in the center. Remove from oven and hot water bath. Uncover and place on a wire rack to cool for at least 10 minutes before unmolding. Serve hot or cold.

Salmon Mousse

Makes about 4 cups

1 pound boneless, skinless fresh
salmon fillet
2 large eggs
1½ cups heavy cream
Coarse salt
White pepper

Chill the bowl and metal blade of a food processor. When they are well chilled, fit them onto the food processor. Chop the salmon, place it in the prepared food processor, and process until very smooth. With processor running, add the eggs and then the cream. Season to taste with salt and pepper.

Use the uncooked mousse as a filling for vegetable roulades or pastas that will be cooked. It may also be used to make quenelles that will be gently poached in a court bouillon.

To use mousse as an appetizer or hors d'oeuvre, place it in a well-buttered 2-quart mold lined with buttered parchment paper. Tightly seal with aluminum foil. Place in a hot-water bath in a preheated 350°F oven and bake for about 20 minutes, or until mousse is cooked in the center. Remove from oven and hot-water bath. Uncover and place on a wire rack to cool for at least 10 minutes before unmolding. Serve hot or cold.

Duck Confit

Serves 6

3 ducks
6 shallots, peeled
5 cloves garlic, peeled
2 bunches fresh parsley
4 bay leaves
Pinch dried thyme
3 tablespoons coarse salt
Lard (optional)

Using a boning knife, separate legs, including thighs, from the ducks. Reserve all fat. Reserve remaining duck pieces for another use. Place duck fat in a medium

sauté pan over low heat. Cook for 15 minutes, or until all of the fat has been rendered out. Strain into a small bowl, discarding solids. Cover and reserve. It is not necessary to refrigerate.

Slice shallots and garlic in a food processor fitted with slicing blade. Place in a mixing bowl. Wash and roughly chop parsley. Combine with garlic and shallots. Crumble bay leaves into mixture. Stir in thyme. Sprinkle half the mixture on the bottom of a large, shallow, nonreactive pan. Sprinkle half of the salt on top. Place legs on top, skin sides up. Sprinkle remaining salt, then remaining seasoning mixture on top of legs. Cover tightly. Lay a heavy pan or cutting board on top and weight down. Refrigerate for 5 days.

Remove legs from seasoning mixture and rub spices off. Place the legs in a heavy saucepan with enough rendered fat to cover. Add lard if there is not enough duck fat. Place over medium heat and cook at a slow simmer for 1½ to 2 hours, or until almost falling apart. Remove from heat and allow to cool in the fat. Place in a ceramic bowl or terrine. Cover and refrigerate for 1 to 2 weeks to allow flavors to develop.

A NOTE FROM JUDIE: Duck confit is based on an ancient Gascogne method of preserving meat. The duck fat serves both as a seal and as a preservative. A well-fatted confit will last, refrigerated, for about 6 months.

Lemon Confit

Makes 1 cup

1 cup sugar
¼ teaspoon coarse salt
8 thick-skinned, blemish-free
lemons

Combine ½ cup of sugar and the salt. Cut the two ends from the lemons. Using a very sharp paring knife, carefully peel the lemons in one continuous turn from the top to the bottom, removing the yellow rind only. Cut the rind into small batons 1 inch long by ¼ inch wide and

place in a nonreactive container. Pour the sugar-salt mixture over the rind and toss to combine. Cover and refrigerate for 3 days.

Lightly rinse rind under cold running water. Combine with 2 cups of water in a small saucepan over medium heat. Bring to a boil. Remove from heat and drain well. Place rind back in the saucepan. Add remaining ½ cup of sugar and 2 cups of water and place over medium-high heat. Bring to a boil. Lower heat and simmer for 45 minutes, or until tender. Remove from heat and pour into a nonreactive container to cool. When cool, cover and refrigerate until ready to use.

Semolina Pasta Dough

Makes about 1 pound

1 cup semolina flour
1 cup bread flour
2 large eggs
½ teaspoon olive oil
1 teaspoon coarse salt or to taste
About ¼ cup ice water

Place the flours, eggs, olive oil, and salt in the bowl of a heavy-duty mixer. Beat at low speed until incorporated. Increase speed and continue to beat until dough is smooth and forms a ball, adding water, a teaspoon at a time, if necessary. Remove from mixer bowl and knead by hand for about 5 minutes, or until smooth.

If you're not using it immediately, wrap dough, airtight, in plastic film, and let it rest at room temperature. Do not refrigerate or allow it to sit for more than 3 hours, or dough will toughen and be unusable.

Following the manufacturer's instructions for your pasta machine, cut dough into pieces and begin thinning and then shaping it into whatever pasta size and shape is called for in your recipe. When recipe requires sheets, roll dough to about 12-inch lengths.

A NOTE FROM JUDIE: Semolina flour, because it has so much tough gluten, is the best flour to use when making pasta to be compressed and shaped by a hand-cranked pasta machine. It also cooks to a perfectly firm-to-the-bite consistency—al dente. Although there are now many electric pasta extruders, the basic hand-cranked machine is used in almost all restaurant kitchens. It is simple to use, easy to maintain, and turns out perfect pasta. Plus, it is perhaps one of the least expensive kitchen aids. You can, of course, make pasta by hand, but it is truly a learned art. If you wish to do so, refer to the books of either Marcella Hazan or Giuliano Bugialli to learn the precise technique.

You can make spinach pasta by combining 1½ cups semolina flour, 2 large eggs, and ½ pound finely chopped, cooked, fresh spinach. Proceed using the directions given above.

Herb-Potato Maximes

Makes about 20

These little works of art add dazzle to the plate, and they are deliciously addictive as well. In the restaurant kitchen, the cooks are forever popping them into their mouths—much to the consternation of whoever has been in charge of baking them for the day. Making one recipe isn't bad, but to make hundreds every day is more than tiresome. This is just a warning—perhaps you had better slice an extra potato for the cook's pleasure!

½ cup Clarified Butter (page 197)
2 large Idaho potatoes
Twenty 1½-inch-long chive points
20 fresh tarragon leaves
20 tiny fresh chervil sprigs
Coarse salt

Preheat oven to 275°F.

Brush a heavy nonstick baking sheet with clarified butter. Set aside.

Peel potatoes. Rinse them under cold running water and pat dry. Slice one potato, lengthwise, on a mandoline or Japanese vegetable slicer, into paper-thin pieces, discarding the end pieces. You should get 18 to 20 even slices from each potato.

Working quickly, lay the potato slices out next to one another, but not touching, on the prepared baking sheet. Place one piece of each herb in an abstract pattern in the center of the potato slice, making sure you have kept a small border all around.

Moving quickly, slice the second potato as described above. Dry the slices slightly and lay them evenly on top of the herb-topped slices. Once all the potatoes are covered, firmly press each "sandwich" together to seal the edges. Brush with remaining butter and season with salt to taste. Place in preheated oven and bake, turning baking sheet from time to time, for 25 minutes, or until golden. Remove from oven and drain on paper towels. Serve at room temperature.

A NOTE FROM JUDIE: You can replace the clarified butter with nonstick vegetable spray, but in doing so, you will lose the sweet-butter taste. To make perfect *maximes*, you must have absolutely flat baking sheets, as any warping will cause the potatoes to pull apart. If your pans are not perfectly flat, spray nonstick vegetable spray on the bottom of another baking sheet of equal size. Place it on top of the potatoes to hold them flat while baking. If you are baking in a convection oven, preheat it to 300°F and bake for a bit less time. Potato *maximes* require careful watching, as once they begin to brown, the process moves quickly. You might want to move them around carefully as the outside *maximes* will usually brown before the inside ones.

Potato Gaufrettes

Makes about 8 per potato

You must use a mandoline to make *gaufrettes*, which are very thin, latticed potato chips baked to a crisp, golden crunch.

Large Idaho potato(es)
About ¼ cup Clarified Butter (page 197) per potato
Coarse salt
Pepper

Scrub the potato(es). Using a very sharp paring knife, carefully shape each potato into a perfect oval. When peeled, place in a bowl of cold water to prevent oxidation.

Preheat oven to 325°F.

Spray a perfectly flat nonstick baking sheet with nonstick vegetable spray. Set aside.

Rest a mandoline on a damp kitchen towel to keep it from slipping. With the bottom blade of the mandoline set at ⅛-inch thickness, run the potato, lengthwise, across the blade to the left on a 45-degree angle. On the next pass, turn the potato to the right and run it, lengthwise, across the blade at a 45-degree angle. Continue making this back-and-forth motion until you come to the end of the potato. You should have about 8 potato thins cut in a lattice design.

Dip them into clarified butter and gently shake to remove any excess. Place them on the prepared baking sheet and season to taste with salt and pepper. Place in preheated oven and bake for 6 minutes, or until golden. Remove from oven and drain on paper towels. Serve hot or at room temperature.

A NOTE FROM JUDIE: Potato *gaufrettes* can be made up to 2 days before using. Store them in an airtight container.

Salsify or Parsnip Chips

Makes about 3 cups

These crispy garnishes can be made up to 2 days in advance. Store them in an airtight container until ready to serve. Reheat them in a preheated 200°F oven for about 5 minutes.

2 large salsify (or parsnips)
Approximately 3 cups unflavored vegetable oil
Coarse salt

Peel and trim salsify or parsnips. Using a vegetable peeler, peel off long, thin shavings. Heat oil in a medium saucepan over medium-high heat until it registers 375°F on a kitchen thermometer. Drop shavings, a few at a time, into hot oil. Fry for about 2 minutes, or until golden and crisp. Using a slotted spoon, remove them from oil and drain them on paper towels. Continue frying and draining until all shavings are cooked. Season to taste with salt. Serve warm.

A NOTE FROM JUDIE: Any root vegetable can be used to make these crispy garnishes.

Crispy Leeks

Makes about 1 cup

Easy to prepare, these can be made early in the day and then reheated for about 5 minutes in a preheated 300°F oven just before serving.

2 leeks
¼ cup vegetable oil
Coarse salt

Trim leeks of all green parts. Cut them in half, lengthwise. Holding each half together, wash all grit away under cold running water. Pat dry with paper towels. Lay each half, cut side down, on a cutting board and slice, lengthwise, into fine julienne. Again, pat dry with paper towels.

Heat the oil in a medium, nonstick sauté pan over medium heat. Add the leek julienne and fry for about 3 minutes, or until golden and crisp. Using a slotted spoon, remove to paper towels and allow to drain well. Season to taste with salt. Serve warm or at room temperature.

A NOTE FROM JUDIE: Don't worry if leeks get soggy—they can be made crisp by reheating. Be sure to lay them out in a single layer when reheating so that they crisp quickly. Make sure the leeks are very clean and very dry before frying. Water will cause oil to splatter and keep leeks soft.

Sherry- or Red Wine–Shallot Vinaigrette

Makes about 1 cup

11 shallots, peeled
¾ cup olive oil
¼ cup finely chopped white onion
¼ cup finely chopped carrot
¼ cup finely chopped celery
¼ cup red wine
¼ cup rich Chicken Stock (see Note, page 189)
1 Sachet (page 197)
¼ cup sherry wine vinegar (or red wine vinegar)
Coarse salt
Pepper
2 tablespoons chopped fresh parsley

Finely mince 5 shallots. Heat ¼ cup of olive oil in a small sauté pan over medium heat. Add minced shallots and sauté for about 5 minutes, or until translucent. Scrape from pan and set aside to cool.

Roughly chop remaining 6 shallots. Combine them with the onion, carrot, and celery. Heat 2 tablespoons of olive oil in a small sauté pan over medium heat. Add chopped vegetables and stir to coat. Lower heat and cook, stirring frequently, for about 4 minutes, or until vegetables are tender. Raise heat to medium and add red wine. Bring to a simmer and allow to simmer for about 5 minutes, or until pan is almost dry. Stir in chicken stock and sachet. Bring to a simmer and allow to simmer for about 4 minutes, or until liquid is reduced by half.

Immediately strain through a fine sieve into a medium-sized heatproof bowl. Discard solids. Allow liquid to cool. When cool, whisk in remaining oil and sherry vinegar. Season to taste with salt and pepper. Stir in reserved minced shallot and parsley just before serving.

NOTE: This vinaigrette has two very different and distinct flavors, depending on whether it is made with red wine or sherry wine. All recipes requiring shallot vinaigrette will specify whether it is Sherry-Shallot or Red Wine–Shallot Vinaigrette.

Citrus Vinaigrette

Makes about 1 cup

3 shallots
1 cup plus 2 tablespoons olive oil
Zest of 3 lemons
½ cup chopped white onion
½ cup chopped celery
2 bay leaves
½ teaspoon freshly grated black peppercorns
½ cup fresh lemon juice
¼ cup rich Chicken Stock (see Note, page 189)
¼ cup white wine vinegar
Coarse salt
Pepper
1 recipe Sweet Lemon Zest (optional; recipe follows)
1 recipe Brunoise of Carrot and Celery (optional; recipe follows)

Peel and chop shallots.

Heat 2 tablespoons of olive oil in a medium sauté pan over medium heat. Stir in shallots, lemon zest, onion, celery, bay leaves, and peppercorns. Lower heat and sauté for about 3 minutes, or until vegetables are tender. Stir in ¼ cup of lemon juice and the chicken stock. Raise heat to medium and bring to a simmer. Simmer for about 5 minutes, or until liquid is reduced by half.

Immediately strain through a fine sieve into a medium-sized heatproof bowl. Discard solids. Allow to cool. When cool, whisk in vinegar and remaining ¼ cup of lemon juice and 1 cup of olive oil. Season to taste with salt and pepper. Stir in the optional sweet lemon zest and *brunoise* of carrot and celery, if using, just before serving.

Sweet Lemon Zest

Makes about 2 tablespoons

1 unblemished lemon
¼ cup sugar
2 tablespoons coarse salt

Remove zest from the lemon and cut it into fine julienne. Combine with remaining ingredients and ½ cup of water in a small saucepan over medium-high heat. Bring to a boil. Lower heat and simmer for 10 minutes, or until zest is very tender. Drain and rinse under cold running water. Pat dry. Use as a garnish in vinaigrettes.

Brunoise of Carrot and Celery

Makes about ½ cup

¼ cup finely minced carrot
¼ cup finely minced celery
1 teaspoon coarse salt

Combine vegetables and salt with cold water to cover in a small saucepan over medium-high heat. Bring to a boil. Lower heat and simmer for 3 minutes, or until vegetables are just tender. Drain and rinse under cold running water. Pat dry. Use as a garnish in vinaigrettes and pan sauces.

Truffle Vinaigrette

Makes about 1 cup

3 ounces truffle peelings (see Note)
¼ cup Madeira wine
½ cup plus 2 tablespoons olive oil
¼ cup chopped white onion
¼ cup chopped carrot
¼ cup chopped celery
1 Sachet (page 197)
¼ cup rich Chicken Stock (see Note, page 189)
¼ cup sherry wine vinegar
¼ cup truffle oil (see Note)
Coarse salt
Pepper
3 tablespoons chopped Fines Herbes (page 197)

Combine truffle peelings and Madeira in a small saucepan over medium heat. Bring to a simmer. Simmer for 5 minutes. Strain through a fine sieve, reserving liquid and peelings separately.

Heat 2 tablespoons of olive oil in same saucepan over medium heat. Add onion, carrot, celery, and sachet. Sauté for about 4 minutes, or until vegetables are tender. Add reserved Madeira and stir to deglaze pan. Continue to cook for about 3 minutes, or until pan is almost dry. Add chicken stock and cook for about 4 minutes, or until liquid is reduced by half. Immediately strain through a fine sieve into a medium-sized heatproof bowl.

Discard solids. Allow liquid to cool. When cool, whisk in vinegar, remaining ½ cup olive oil, and the truffle oil. Season to taste with salt and pepper. Stir in the herbs just before serving.

NOTE: Truffle oil and truffle peelings are ready-made products available at specialty-food stores or through one of the mail-order sources listed on page 199.

Curry Vinaigrette

Makes about 1 cup

½ cup plus 2 tablespoons olive oil
¼ cup chopped onion
¼ cup chopped carrot
¼ cup chopped celery
1 Sachet (page 197)
¼ cup white wine
2 tablespoons curry powder
1 tablespoon ground turmeric
½ cup rich Chicken Stock (see Note, page 189)
¼ cup white wine vinegar
Coarse salt
Pepper
1 tablespoon chopped fresh herbs, or 2 tablespoons finely diced fresh papaya or melon (optional)

Heat 2 tablespoons of olive oil in a small saucepan over medium heat. Add onion, carrot, celery, and sachet. Sauté for about 4 minutes, or until vegetables are tender. Add the white wine, curry, and turmeric and continue to cook for about

4 minutes, or until the pan is almost dry. Add the chicken stock and bring to a simmer. Simmer for about 5 minutes, or until liquid is reduced by half. Immediately strain through a fine sieve into a medium-sized heatproof bowl.

Discard solids. Allow liquid to cool. When cool, slowly whisk in the remaining ½ cup of olive oil. As mixture begins to emulsify, begin to alternately add vinegar with the oil to create a very thick vinaigrette. Season to taste with salt and pepper. Just before serving, stir in optional herbs, papaya, or melon.

A NOTE FROM CHARLIE: I make this vinaigrette a bit thicker than usual. If it gets too thick, I whisk in warm water, a drop at a time. The optional herbs or fruit are not necessary but add a colorful touch and nice texture to the plate.

Mustard Vinaigrette

Makes about 3½ cups

¼ cup rich Chicken Stock (see Note, page 189)
1 tablespoon Dijon mustard
1 teaspoon dry mustard
1 cup rice wine vinegar (see Note)
2 cups olive oil
½ cup mustard oil (see Note)
1 teaspoon coarse salt or to taste
½ teaspoon freshly ground white pepper or to taste

Place chicken stock in a small saucepan over medium heat. Bring to a boil. Lower heat and simmer for 4 minutes, or until reduced to 2 tablespoons. Remove from the heat and allow to cool.

Combine reduced chicken stock, Dijon mustard, dry mustard, and rice wine vinegar. When well blended, whisk in olive and mustard oils. Season to taste with salt and pepper. If not using immediately, store, covered and refrigerated, until ready to serve.

NOTE: Rice wine vinegar is available in Asian markets and some specialty stores.

Mustard oil is available from Zabar's or other fine specialty-food stores (see Sources, page 199).

Balsamic Vinaigrette

Makes about 1½ cups

½ cup plus 2 tablespoons olive oil
¼ cup chopped white onion
¼ cup chopped carrot
¼ cup chopped celery
4 shallots, peeled and finely
    chopped
2 cloves garlic, peeled and finely
    chopped
2 bay leaves
½ teaspoon freshly cracked black
    pepper
½ cup rich Chicken Stock (see
    Note, page 189)
½ cup balsamic vinegar
Coarse salt and pepper to taste
2 tablespoons chopped fresh
    parsley

Heat 2 tablespoons olive oil in a small saucepan over medium heat. Add onion. carrot, celery, shallots, garlic, bay leaves, and pepper. Sauté for about 4 minutes or until vegetables are tender. Add chicken stock and ¼ cup vinegar and bring to a simmer. Simmer for about 5 minutes, or until liquid is reduced by one half. Immediately strain through a fine sieve into a medium-sized heat-proof bowl. Discard solids. Allow liquid to cool.

When cool, gently stir in remaining olive oil and vinegar. Do not emulsify. Season to taste with salt and pepper. Stir in minced parsley just before serving.

Tomato Vinaigrette

Makes about 1 cup

6 cloves garlic
4 shallots
2 tablespoons olive oil
¼ cup canned tomato puree
¼ cup chopped Spanish onion
¼ cup chopped celery
2 tablespoons chopped fresh basil
1 tablespoon chopped fresh oregano
2 bay leaves
½ teaspoon freshly cracked black
    pepper

¼ cup red wine
½ cup rich Chicken Stock (see
    page 189)
1 cup Tomato Oil (see page 196)
½ cup red wine vinegar
Coarse salt to taste
2 tablespoons finely diced, peeled,
    seeded plum tomato
1 tablespoon julienned fresh basil
    leaves

Peel and chop garlic and shallots.

Heat olive oil in a small saucepan over medium heat. Add chopped garlic and shallots, tomato puree, onion, celery, chopped basil, oregano, bay leaves, and pepper. Stir to coat. Lower heat and sauté for about 5 minutes, or until vegetables are translucent. Add red wine and stir to deglaze pan. Continue to cook for about 4 minutes, or until pan is almost dry, being careful not to burn pan. Add chicken stock and cook, stirring constantly, for about 5 minutes, or until liquid is reduced by one half. Immediately strain through a fine sieve, pushing to extract all liquid. Discard solids. Allow liquid to cool. When cool, whisk in tomato oil and vinegar until just barely combined. Taste and adjust seasoning with salt and pepper. Stir in diced tomato and julienned basil just before serving.

A NOTE FROM CHARLIE: This vinaigrette should not be thickly emulsified. You want to achieve a rather broken, marble-like effect on the plate.

Spicy Red Onion Marmalade

Makes about 3 cups

¾ cup Sauternes
3 tablespoons fresh lemon juice
¼ cup maple syrup
¼ cup plus 2 tablespoons honey
1 cinnamon stick
2 tablespoons olive oil
1 ½ cups diced red bell pepper
4 large red onions, peeled and
    diced

1 jalapeño chile, stemmed and
    minced
½ teaspoon coarse salt

Place Sauternes, lemon juice, maple syrup, ¼ cup honey, and cinnamon stick in a heavy saucepan over medium-high heat. Bring to a simmer. Lower heat and cook, stirring frequently, for about 15 minutes, or until a thick syrup has formed. Set aside.

Heat 1 tablespoon oil in a medium sauté pan over medium heat. Add diced pepper and sauté for about 5 minutes, or until soft. Add 1 tablespoon honey and stir to coat. Remove from heat and set aside.

Heat remaining oil in a large sauté pan over medium heat. Add onions, jalapeño, remaining honey, and salt. Cook, stirring frequently, for about 15 minutes. Add cooked peppers and three quarters of the reserved syrup. Cook, stirring frequently, for about 15 minutes, or until quite thick and jamlike. Remove from heat. Puree one half of the mixture and the remaining syrup in a food processor fitted with the metal blade. Stir pureed half into the jam and stir to combine. Return to heat and cook for 5 minutes. Scrape from pan into nonreactive bowl and allow to cool. Store, covered and refrigerated, for up to 1 month.

A NOTE FROM CHARLIE: This marmalade can be used as a garnish for meats or game or as a condiment to make an interesting sandwich.

Red Wine Mignonette

Makes about 1 cup

1 bunch fresh parsley
2 tablespoons olive oil
½ cup chopped shallots
2 tablespoons freshly cracked
  black peppercorns
1 bay leaf
½ cup red wine
½ cup red wine vinegar
¼ cup grapeseed oil
8 whole shallots
Coarse salt
Pepper

Wash and dry parsley. Pick off leaves and reserve leaves and stems separately.

Heat the olive oil in a small saucepan over medium heat. Add chopped shallots, reserved parsley stems, peppercorns, and bay leaf. Reduce heat to very low and allow shallots to just barely cook for about 15 minutes, or until very translucent. Add the wine, vinegar, and grapeseed oil. Raise heat and bring to a boil. Lower heat and simmer for 15 minutes.

Meanwhile, peel and finely mince whole shallots. Place them in a heatproof, nonreactive bowl. Strain hot mixture over the minced shallots. Discard solids. Allow liquid to cool. When cool, season to taste with salt and pepper.

Tomato Oil

Makes about 1½ cups

4 cloves garlic
1 ½ cups plus 2 tablespoons olive oil
¼ cup chopped white onion
¼ cup chopped celery
2 tablespoons chopped fresh basil
1 tablespoon chopped fresh
  oregano
2 bay leaves
½ cup canned tomato puree

Peel and chop garlic.

Heat ¼ cup of olive oil in a small saucepan over medium heat. Add chopped garlic, onion, celery, basil, oregano, and bay leaves. Sauté for 4 minutes, or until vegetables are tender. Add tomato puree. Lower heat and cook, stirring constantly, for 15 minutes. Then, add remaining olive oil and cook, stirring occasionally, for 20 minutes. Remove from heat and set aside for at least 8 hours to allow the oil to rise to the top.

Using a small ladle, remove the tomato-flavored oil, being careful not to disturb the solids that have settled on the bottom of the pan. Discard the solids. Pour the oil into a nonreactive container. Cover and refrigerate for up to 2 weeks.

A NOTE FROM JUDIE: Tomato oil can be used as a flavoring for vinaigrettes or to garnish a finished plate.

Chive Oil

Makes about 1 cup

4 ounces fresh chives
1 cup grapeseed oil
Coarse salt
Pepper

Place the chives in rapidly boiling water. Immediately drain and refresh them under cold running water. Pat them dry and roughly chop. Place in a blender with 1 tablespoon of cold water. Process until just pureed. Do not overprocess, as the bright green color will fade. Scrape puree into a small bowl. Whisk in the oil and season with salt and pepper. Pour into a nonreactive container. Cover and refrigerate for up to 3 days. Longer storage will cause the oil to darken but will not harm the flavor.

A NOTE FROM CHARLIE: I like the rough texture of this oil. However, if you want a clear, green oil, allow the oil to drain slowly through a very fine sieve or *chinois*, or pour it through a double layer of cheesecloth, tie the cheesecloth into a bundle, and hang it over a bowl to drain slowly. Chive oil can be used to garnish a finished plate.

Crêpes

Makes about 10

2 large eggs
3 large egg yolks
1 ⅓ cups milk
¼ cup (½ stick) plus 1 tablespoon
  salted butter, melted
1 cup all-purpose flour
Coarse salt
Freshly ground white pepper
Approximately 2 tablespoons Clarified Butter (page 197)

Whisk eggs and egg yolks together. Set aside.

Heat milk in a small saucepan over low heat until just warm. Add melted butter. Then, slowly whisk into eggs.

Place flour and salt and pepper to taste in a mixing bowl. Slowly whisk egg mixture into the flour. When blended, strain through a fine sieve and set aside to rest for at least 1 hour but no more than 6 hours.

Preheat a crêpe pan over medium heat. Brush with clarified butter.

Stir the crêpe batter. If it is thicker than heavy cream, thin it with milk, a teaspoon at a time.

When the butter is very hot but not brown, lift the pan off the heat and ladle in the batter. Quickly tilt the pan so that the batter lightly covers the bottom of the pan. If holes appear, pour in just enough additional batter to cover.

Return the pan to the heat. If batter is of the right consistency and the pan is hot enough, the crêpe will set immediately and it will take about 1 minute for the bottom to brown lightly. Use your fingers to pick up an edge to check for browning. Shake the pan back and forth to keep the crêpe from sticking.

When the crêpe bottom is lightly browned, flip it over and cook for 30 seconds. As each crêpe is cooked, turn it out onto a clean kitchen towel or paper towel. Continue buttering the pan and cooking crêpes until all the batter is used.

If crêpes are to be used immediately, stack them on a warm plate. Cover and keep warm in a very low oven.

If crêpes are made early in the day of use, cool them on a clean kitchen towel. Stack them, with a sheet of waxed or parchment paper in between each crêpe. Cover and store at room temperature until ready to use.

If crêpes are to be frozen for later use, stack them as described in the preceding paragraph. Wrap them tightly in plastic film and then in freezer wrap or a sealed plastic bag. To defrost, unwrap and let stand at room temperature. Do not separate until all the crêpes are thawed or they will break apart.

Clarified Butter

Makes about 3 cups

Clarified butter is simply unsalted butter that has been melted and had the water and milk solids separated out. When used for sautéing, it can withstand higher cooking temperatures without burning than can whole butter.

2 pounds unsalted butter

Place butter in a medium saucepan over very low heat. Cook for 25 minutes. Using a ladle, skim off the white frothy matter as the butter melts, leaving as much of the yellow butterfat as possible. Increase heat to medium and continue to skim off white matter until the top of the melted fat is clear. This should take about 30 minutes. Remove from heat and let stand for 10 minutes.

Skim off any solid material and carefully pour yellow fat into a container with a lid, taking care not to get any of the solid matter from the bottom of the pan. Store, tightly covered and refrigerated, for up to 1 month.

A NOTE FROM JUDIE: Freeze clarified butter only in a pinch. The freezing process puts water back into the butter and changes its heat resistance.

Sachet

A sachet, or *bouquet garni*, is a group of herbs tied together or placed in a cheesecloth bag to be used to flavor sauces, soups, or stews. The tying or bagging facilitates herbs' easy removal from the pot. The traditional mix is parsley, thyme, and bay leaf. When my recipes call for a sachet, you will need a bunch of parsley stems about the size of your little finger, 10 peppercorns, 1 teaspoon dried thyme, and 2 bay leaves tied in a cheesecloth bag.

Fines Herbes

This is a mixture of equal portions of finely chopped fresh chervil, parsley, tarragon, and chives often added to sauces just before service to impart a fresh herb flavor. You can also purchase premixed, dried *fines herbes*, but they can't compare to a fresh mixture.

My recipes calling for *fines herbes* will require 1 teaspoon of each of the herbs mentioned above.

Roasted Garlic

Garlic may be roasted whole, cut in half, crosswise, or separated into individual cloves. To enhance the aromatic sweetness of garlic, it is always roasted at a very low temperature, as high heat will cause it to caramelize too quickly and turn bitter.

Preheat oven to 200°F.

Tightly wrap garlic in aluminum foil. Place it on a small baking sheet in preheated oven. Bake for about 1 hour for whole bulbs, 30 minutes for halved bulbs, and 15 minutes for individual cloves, or until flesh is very soft and deep gold. Remove from oven and allow to rest until cool enough to handle.

To remove garlic from the skins: Using a very sharp knife, cut whole bulb in half, crosswise, and gently force "jam" out by pushing on the closed end. For individual cloves, use a very sharp knife to slit skin open on each clove. Gently force "jam" out of the hole. Discard skin.

To make roasted-garlic puree: For every 6 cloves roasted garlic, blend in 1 tablespoon of extra-virgin olive oil. You can use a fork for a small batch or process larger amounts in a small food processor fitted with the metal blade.

Brunoise

Brunoise is a French culinary term meaning "to cut vegetables into a minute dice," as well as the resulting diced vegetables, which are usually sautéed in clarified butter to just soften. The *brunoise* is then added to finished sauces or soups to provide additional flavor. I most always use the term to describe finely diced vegetables, steamed or cooked in salted water until crisp-tender. Shocked in ice water and patted dry, they are then added to flavor a sauce or vinaigrette just before service.

When a recipe does not specify the type of *brunoise*, it will be calling for equal amounts of carrot, celery, and leek. *Brunoise* is generally prepared just before it is needed so that the vegetables retain maximum flavor.

Mirepoix

Mirepoix is a classic culinary term for a mixture of equal amounts of finely diced carrot, onion, and celery, often seasoned with minced herbs, and sautéed in butter until just softened. Occasionally, cubes of ham or bacon are added to the vegetables to impart a richer flavor. A *mirepoix* is used either to season stews, soups, sauces, and fricassees or as a base for braising meats or fish. Throughout this book, *mirepoix* will refer to equal parts of finely diced carrot, onion, and celery.

A Note about Wedgwood

Throughout this book, and in my restaurant, I use Wedgwood china. I like Wedgwood for two reasons. First because it is classic in design and the china itself is the whitest made. As you can see from the many dishes photographed in this book, Wedgwood patterns enhance the beauty and excitement of my food without ever dominating it. The second reason is practical. The china I use in my restaurant must endure the most rigorous handling imaginable. I've found Wedgwood to be one of the strongest products on the market. Bone china is actually the most durable dinnerware you can buy.

Charlie Palmer

Wedgwood China Patterns

Aureole Wedgwood.
pages 39, 43, and 115

Aztec. *page 173*

Chadwick. *page 141*

Citrons. *page 149*

Clio. *page 132*

Colonade. *page 57*

Cornucopia. *page 35*

Countryware. *pages 77 and 107*

Crown Emerald. *page 33*

Crown Ruby. *pages 6 and 150*

Eden. *page 138*

Fairfield. *page 83*

Festivity. *pages 29, 75, and 121*

Humming Birds. *page 23*

Mistral. *pages 46 and 156*

Nantucket Basket. *page 103*

Osborne. *pages 68 and 112*

Strawberry & Vine. *page 51*

Watercolor. *page 137*

Whitfield. *page 96*

AUX DELICE DE BOIS, INC.
4 Leonard Street
New York, NY 10013
(800) 666-1232
(212) 334-1230
Fax: (212) 334-1231

BALDUCCI'S MAIL ORDER DIVISION
1102 Queens Plaza South
Long Island City, NY 11101
(800) BALDUCCI

BRIDGE KITCHENWARE
214 East 52nd Street
New York, NY 10022
(212) 688-4220
Fax: (212) 758-5387

CERVENA® CO.
780 Third Avenue
Suite 1904
New York, NY 10017
(800) 877-1187
Fax: (212) 832-7602
(natural tender venison from New
Zealand)

CHOCOLATE GALLERY
34 West 22nd Street
New York, NY 10010
(212) 675-2253

D'ARTAGNAN
399–419 Saint Paul Avenue
Jersey City, NJ 07306
(800) DAR-TAGN
(201) 792-0748
Fax: (201) 792-0113

DEAN & DELUCA
560 Broadway
New York, NY 10012
(212) 431-1691
(800) 221-7714

EGG FARM DAIRY
2 John Walsh Boulevard
Peekskill, NY 10566
(800) CREAMERY
Fax: (914) 734-9287
(cultured butter, clabbered cream,
and wild-ripened cheeses)

THE ORIENTAL PANTRY
423 Great Road
Acton, MA 01720
(800) 828-0368
Fax: (617) 275-4506

SULTAN'S DELIGHT
P.O. Box 090302
Brooklyn, NY 11209
(718) 745-6844

WEDGWOOD
1330 Campus Parkway
Wall, NJ 07719
(908) 938-5800

ZABAR'S
2245 Broadway
New York, NY 10024
(212) 787-2000

SOURCES

INDEX

ABOUT THE AUTHORS

——

A native of Smyrna, New York, CHARLIE PALMER, at thirty-six, is the chef and owner of Aureole, Alva, and Lennox Room in Manhattan, and of the Egg Farm Dairy, an upstate creamery, where he produces cheese and butter which *The New York Times* has called "the best in America." In 1993, *Wine Spectator* selected him as one of America's best young chefs of the year. Aureole Restaurant was elected to the Relais & Château society in 1996.

JUDITH CHOATE is a writer, chef, and pioneer in the promotion of American food. A member of the James Beard Foundation, the American Institute of Food and Wine, and the International Association of Culinary Professionals, she owned and operated a retail food shop and catering business in New York City until 1985. She has published fifteen books, including *The Ubiquitous Shrimp*, *Hot!*, and three books in the American Kitchen Classic series, one of which was selected as one of the best cookbooks of 1992.

ABOUT THE TYPE

——

This book was set in Bauer Bodoni, a typeface based on Bodoni, which was designed by the renowned Italian printer and type designer Giambattista Bodoni (1740–1813). Bodoni originally based his letter forms on those of the Frenchman Fournier, and created his type to have beautiful contrasts between light and dark.